Continuing Professional Education of Highly-Qualified Personnel

Ministry of Education & Training
MET Library
13th Floor, Mowat Block, Queen's Park
Toronto   M7A 1L2

ORGANISATION FOR ECONOMIC CO-OPERATION AND DEVELOPMENT

ORGANISATION FOR ECONOMIC CO-OPERATION AND DEVELOPMENT

Pursuant to Article 1 of the Convention signed in Paris on 14th December 1960, and which came into force on 30th September 1961, the Organisation for Economic Co-operation and Development (OECD) shall promote policies designed:

— to achieve the highest sustainable economic growth and employment and a rising standard of living in Member countries, while maintaining financial stability, and thus to contribute to the development of the world economy;
— to contribute to sound economic expansion in Member as well as non-member countries in the process of economic development; and
— to contribute to the expansion of world trade on a multilateral, non-discriminatory basis in accordance with international obligations.

The original Member countries of the OECD are Austria, Belgium, Canada, Denmark, France, Germany, Greece, Iceland, Ireland, Italy, Luxembourg, the Netherlands, Norway, Portugal, Spain, Sweden, Switzerland, Turkey, the United Kingdom and the United States. The following countries became Members subsequently through accession at the dates indicated hereafter: Japan (28th April 1964), Finland (28th January 1969), Australia (7th June 1971), New Zealand (29th May 1973) and Mexico (18th May 1994). The Commission of the European Communities takes part in the work of the OECD (Article 13 of the OECD Convention).

Publié en français sous le titre :
LA FORMATION CONTINUE DES PERSONNELS HAUTEMENT QUALIFIÉS

378
.013
C762

© OECD 1995
Applications for permission to reproduce or translate all or part
of this publication should be made to:
Head of Publications Service, OECD
2, rue André-Pascal, 75775 PARIS CEDEX 16, France.

Foreword

When the Education Committee decided to include a project on "Higher Education and Employment: The Changing Relationship", in its programme of work for 1988-1992, national representatives discussed detailed proposals on three areas of activity for which outlines had been prepared by the Secretariat:
- «The Flows of Graduates from Higher Education and their Entry into Working Life» (four volumes and a synthesis published in 1992-93);
- «The Case of the Humanities and Social Sciences» (published in 1993);
- «Recent Developments in Continuing Professional Education», the current volume.

This publication is a synthesis of the contributions of seventeen OECD countries: Australia, Austria, Canada, Denmark, France, Finland, Germany (the then Federal Republic of Germany), Italy, Japan, the Netherlands, Norway, Portugal, Sweden, Switzerland, the United Kingdom, the United States and the former Yugoslavia.* Two contributions are concerned with open and distance education: Germany and the Commission of the European Communities.

This report by the Secretariat presents an analysis of the situation of continuing professional education of highly-qualified personnel in the various Member countries. While making no claims to compare, it does reveal the features specific to each country, and places them within more general models of continuing education and higher education. Teaching, health and agriculture were excluded *a priori* from the field of investigation either because they were already the subject of other activities, or because they warranted an in-depth and special approach.

The project was led by Danielle Colardyn of the Secretariat. The views expressed do not commit either the OECD or the national authorities concerned. This report is published on the responsibility of the Secretary-General of the OECD.

---

* The national reports are available free, upon request. Please contact Danielle Colardyn of the Directorate for Education, Employment, Labour and Social Affairs, OECD.

Table of contents

Introduction

Background: the changing relationship between higher education and continuing education	10
• Structural change	11
• Demographic trends	11
• Increased participation in higher education	11
• Rising educational level	12
Scope and outline of the report	12

Chapter I
Towards a More Vocationally-Oriented Continuing Education

The emergence of recurrent education	15
• From a social philosophy to economic imperatives	15
• Developments outside the formal system	16
Mass continuing education	17
• The situation of adults	18
The emergence of continuing professional education	18
Diversified higher education	19
The emergence of other educational sectors	21
Relations with the economic environment	22
Closing remarks	23
Notes	24

Chapter II
Segmentation of Continuing Professional Education

Defining the providers	25
• Enterprises: internal markets and human resource management	26
• Professional associations	31
• The commercial sector: attempting a definition	36
• Unions	38
• Non-profit associations	39
• Higher education	39
• Non-university higher education	45
• Open and distance education	47
Other criteria determining the segmentation	48
• Funding	48
• Education and training levels	50
• Discipline	50
• Sectors of professional activity	51
The three market sectors	51
• The formal sector	53
• The non-formal sector	53
• The commercial sector	53
How the training market functions	54
The public authorities and the training market functioning	56
• A traditionally centralised context	56
• A traditionally decentralised context	57
• A market context	59
Benefits and limitations	62
Notes	62

Chapter III
Towards a Continuing Professional Education Policy in Higher Education

Which continuing professional education?	63
• Single-subject courses	64
• Commissioned education	65
• Personnel education under the auspices of higher education	65
• "Advanced programmes"	67
Implications for higher education institutions	72
• Access	72
• Certification	73
• Funding	79
• Curbs on development	83
The roles of higher education in the training market	84

Chapter IV
Five Challenges for the Future

Diversified demand and targeted supply	87
Training for the private sector without losing specificities	87
Competition and the market	87
Co-ordinating initial and continuing education	88
Initiating a new social dialogue	89
Annex 1: Statistical Information	91
Annex 2: National Contributions	99
Bibliography	103

Introduction

This study examines recent developments in the continuing professional education of highly-qualified personnel, and focuses on their implications for higher education policies. It aims to define the activities covered by continuing professional education, to distinguish them from adult education, and to identify the roles and missions of higher education in this context. Continuing professional education excludes adult education and recurrent or remedial education, even if the functions of higher education establishments cover these.

Highly-qualified personnel are defined either by their initial higher education, their membership in a professional body (licensing), or by their professional functions and responsibilities. The term "continuing education", however, is used broadly to include educational activities targeting highly-qualified personnel whose professions require that they update their skills and knowledge.

In order to examine this aspect of adult continuing education, the roles of all public and private providers in the training market, including institutions of higher education, employers and professional associations, were analysed. The goal is to situate continuing professional education developed in higher education within the general context of training offered in the market. The term "market" recurs throughout this report and needs some clarification because it cannot be used or interpreted in a strictly economic sense. For continuing education there is no outright competition among providers, and demand is somewhat ill-defined while information is comparatively accessible. Moreover, the market does not function on a true cost basis because institutions of higher education do not operate on commercial principles, and the continuing professional education they provide is generally partially financed with public funds. Notwithstanding these problems, the broad notion of "market" helps us consider and understand recent developments in continuing professional education, and the roles and missions of institutions of higher education in providing continuing education for highly-qualified personnel. At the same time, the term "market" accurately conveys the existence of multiple and specialised providers; their attempts to establish relationships; their degree of competitiveness; the place and role of institutions of higher education, for whom the consequences of this emerging competition in continuing professional education has implications for their current primary missions.

Background: the changing relationship between higher education and continuing education

The issues now facing the world of education are upsetting the traditional balance between general and vocational education, between initial training and continuing education, and between formal education and "experiential learning" which are affecting the entire course of individuals' social, cultural and working lives. Country contributions have looked at the situation from the economic perspective of the late 1980s, while in 1990-92 the economic recession has worsened rapidly. This report is based therefore on a commercial sector in a booming economy. Several countries are currently going through turbulent structural changes which have already affected continuing professional education and its links with the working world.

The significant change apparent in recent years is the growing proportion of service jobs. Generally speaking, the structure of skills and competences in the working population has progressed, and, more specifically, the nature of work has changed. Human resources have been recognised as crucial for running enterprises, for production and for economic competitiveness but their management is complex. Required skills, like working conditions, are changing as jobs disappear and new opportunities emerge. Job diversification is daily becoming more apparent (OECD, 1990*a*).

In addition, the nature of knowledge and advances in science and technology are now making initial acquired expertise rapidly obsolete. A continuing education strategy and, more precisely, a continuing professional strategy are necessary, for without continuing education it is difficult to augment knowledge or transfer expertise and technological know-how. The pace of this growth favours a more highly-qualified labour force which alone is capable of coping with increasing job complexity.

A continuing professional education strategy must be long-term as well. For while immediate requirements must be met, long-term needs cannot be ignored. The demand for continuing education and continuing professional education, already highly developed in the leading-edge sectors, will grow. To encourage innovation, a more strategic view has to be taken which includes a genuine long-term policy involving different providers. Institutions of higher education must be considered among the providers, for they in particular lay the foundations for the requisite innovative capacity by supplying the tools for acquiring expertise, and by offering an individual lifelong access to a variety of disciplines.

General economic conditions and labour market trends demand a long-term vision of continuing education for both workers at risk and the highly-qualified population. The fact that continuing education is growing helps those parts of the population at greatest risk of social and vocational alienation to maintain or improve their vocational status. In the case of the most highly qualified, it helps maintain and develop knowledge and competences (OECD, 1988, 1991*a*, 1991*b*).

The educational sectors concur on the range of factors contributing to the growth and current developments in the continuing professional education of highly-qualified personnel. Without going into great detail, we will emphasize: the role of structural change; demography; increased participation in higher education; the general increase in the educational level of the population.

Structural change

Technological and organisational trends call for a new type of management which can not only adapt to changes, but can generate, create, and pave the way for them. Productivity in the labour force, including the most highly-qualified workers, is closely linked to its flexibility, and is essential for accepting, managing, and even generating structural change and its organisational corollaries. Continuing education will encourage transfers of technological expertise and dissemination of scientific knowledge in order to prepare managerial staff for the new dimensions of their functions.

Current structural change makes plain the need to develop continuing education at every level, and in every sector. This involves an increasing number of workers and individuals, whether continuing education is general, vocational or second-chance, or, as we shall see in this study, professional education of highly-qualified personnel.

Demographic trends

Member countries advance other arguments to justify the current growth of continuing professional education: decelerated growth of the working-age population, and the shrinkage of the 15-24 age group. It is a fact that there will be approximately 20 per cent fewer 16 year-olds in 2002 than in 1982, which will probably reduce the size of the group chiefly targeted by higher level education and training. At the same time, some countries forecast highly qualified labour shortages. In Switzerland, for example, a survey conducted in 1988 revealed that 48 per cent of the enterprises consulted complained of a lack of qualified personnel (Swiss Authorities, 1989).

In the future, education and training systems might place young persons on the labour market at an earlier age. This will generate increased demand for short-term "updating" training targeting those already at work, and young persons having completed short degrees in higher education.

Several countries participating in the "Higher Education and Employment" activity stress the gravity of the demographic problems for the volume and nature of the demand for education and training (Netherlands, Austria). In the near future, the qualifications and competences of the entire population will have to be sustained and developed to respond to structural changes and demographic trends.

Increased participation in higher education

All countries make the point that there are increasing numbers of young persons in higher education and they foresee a continued trend in coming years (Sweden, Denmark, France). Currently, higher education is important for young persons to acquire qualifications. Participation rates have risen considerably over the last fifteen to twenty years. The trend for 20-24 year-olds entering university and non-university higher education between 1975 and 1986 lets us divide Member countries into three groups according to whether participation rose by 50 per cent or over, by 25-45 per cent, or by 12-19 per cent (OECD, 1990*b*). In 1988, participation rates based on the 20-24 age group in most countries were 20-40 per cent, with a high of about 50 per cent and a low around 20 per cent (*cf.* Table A.1, Annex 1).

Not only will young people increasingly demand initial higher education in the 1990s, but so will the older population. Between now and the end of the century, access to higher education (the *numerus clausus* problem in Sweden and Denmark, and conversely "unlimited access", for example in France) must be redefined. Increased numbers of students in higher education will increase participation in continuing professional education, especially because at the same time that large numbers of young persons begin initial higher education, short-term diplomas (France, Sweden, the United States) are being introduced. Ten years or so from now, these same young people will need continuing professional education as a means of confronting sharper international competition. That higher education opens up at the same time that continuing education expands presents a major dilemma and a substantial difficulty for higher education in the years to come.

Rising educational level

It follows from this that the educational level of the population is rising. The 1989 OECD survey of the educational attainment of the labour force showed a rising proportion of persons with a post-secondary or higher level education (OECD, 1989*a*). Examining the percentage of the population with at least a partial post-secondary education, without a degree (Level D) or with a degree (Level E, at least a university degree) indicates the percentage of the labour force targeted by continuing professional education considered throughout this report (Table A.2, Annex 1). These data were available for ten countries in 1988. For seven of these, from approximately 20 per cent to 40 per cent of the labour force are potentially affected by the continuing professional education considered here. In the other three countries, the figure is below 10 per cent.

Despite the paucity of refined quantitative data relating to high levels of qualification, it seems reasonable to believe that the presence of highly-qualified personnel with or without a degree in the qualification structure of the labour force is tending to increase and is likely to grow over the next decade.

Scope and outline of the report

This report, drawn from the Member country contributions (see Annex 2), examines how educational policies and, more particularly, higher education policies, can cope with the consequences of the growth and diversification of the market of continuing professional education for highly-qualified personnel.

The global trends discussed above affect initial and continuing education and training systems as well as the roles and missions of higher education. The term "continuing education for highly-qualified personnel" is broadly used in this project to include university and non-university education, and shorter and advanced degrees. If necessary, and where possible, a distinction will be made between institutional components and educational levels: university and non-university, distance education, and open universities. If the missions of distance education and open universities were long directed more towards "second-chance" continuing education than towards the continuing professional education of employed highly-qualified personnel, various examples emphasize a change. Continuing professional education occupies a growing place here (Department of Pharmacy, 1992).

Associated problems are very specific: providers in the training market are highly specialised and quite distinct from those involved in continuing adult education; public authorities and their private partners have very special roles to play; funding arrangements are governed by criteria differing from those applied in adult education in general; certifying and recognising professional skills have a very direct bearing on the human resource management policies implemented by enterprises. Moreover, the population of highly-qualified personnel targeted by this project falls into occupational categories which vary from country to country, and change over the span of a career, since professional experience more than initial degrees tends to define functions. What is more, on-the-job learning has always been recognised as an important part of continuing education, even for highly-qualified personnel and it is currently growing and gaining increasing recognition (Eurich, 1990; Cervero and Azzeretto, 1990).

Should higher education policies consider the whole range of growing developments, which have given rise to the non-formal and commercial sectors (sometimes called the "third sectory")? To what extent can the policies of formal education systems integrate, assimilate, and evolve in response to external economic developments? What are the potential consequences of these developments for initial higher education? Answers will be sketched on the basis of discernible general trends in the Member countries.

Chapter I examines the changes in the demand for continuing education in order to provide a context for considering the development of the various components over the last twenty years and for analysing the significance of the growth of continuing education within the framework of higher education (adult participation, part-time studies, distance education, and institutional diversifications).

Chapter II considers what continuing professional education is offered, how it is segmented and how it functions in formal, non-formal and commercial sectors, and the roles of public authorities with regard to the market.

Chapter III is concerned with the consequences and challenges for institutions of higher education, given recent developments in continuing professional education for access, certification, funding, and curbs on development.

Chapter IV examines the challenges for the future.

Chapter I

Towards a More Vocationally-Oriented Continuing Education

The emergence of recurrent education

Increased and changing demands for continuing education and continuing professional education mean that more adults with more intensely occupational needs are involved. They are turning to higher education. In response, these institutions are opening up and diversifying their roles and missions.

For more than two decades, continuing education and continuing professional education have been constant concerns in Member countries who have repeatedly affirmed the need for a lifelong educational process. As defined by the OECD in the early 1970s, recurrent education essentially aimed at initiating new educational possibilities. Rather than a system which educated youths in one stretch, lifelong education would alternate with other activities, in particular with work (OECD, 1975). These were not new educational objectives, but a reconsideration of education's temporal logic.

From a social philosophy to economic imperatives

The terms recurrent, adult, lifelong, continuing and continuing professional education are often interchangeable and reflect more or less similar situations today, depending on the Member country. The OECD proposed different definitions in the 1970s (OECD, 1975 and 1977). Its 1975 study identified trends in the issues affecting continuing education, at a time when arguments of justice and social equity held centre stage. Certain social concerns were evident:

a) Continuing education was perceived as a means of modifying certain shortcomings of initial training that did not create equal opportunity. This attitude stressed the notion of positive discrimination and remedial action between generations.

b) Continuing education was proposed as a means of combating the accelerated obsolescence of knowledge.

c) Emulation between the systems of initial and continuing education was seen as having a positive effect on the development of initial training.

d) The relationship to employment was expressed in terms of "industrial democracy, job security and improved career prospects for the individual".

During the 1970s, the principles underpinning continuing education made more reference to initial education than to employment. The continuing education system would dynamise initial education which had failed to provide equality of opportunity because its structures did not enable theory to be linked to practice and because its curricula did not keep pace with the changes taking place in the world of work.

It is immediately apparent that the initial situation has changed.[1] Some of the egalitarian considerations of the 1970s have receded into the background, or have become part of a broader strategy linked to the career concept. There now exists a collective awareness of the implications of continuing education as an aspect of work; worries about productivity, innovation, competitiveness and employment are vital and persuasive arguments for continuing education. For the most disadvantaged, this is generally thanks to public authorities. But for more qualified personnel, private actors are appearing on the scene, and the roles of enterprises and professional associations become apparent.

Recurrent Education (OECD, 1975) presented the stakes behind the two approaches to continuing education beginning to take shape. The first approach looked at recurrent education as an individual right, while the second saw it as a means of satisfying the requirements of a changing society by increasing available work-related education and therefore the knowledge, skills, and mobility of the labour force.

Between 1975 and 1990, the notion of training as an "individual right" shifted: education and training became economic and social necessities, in which everyone shared responsibility. The occupational orientation largely reflected changes in the balance of power between social partners.

The keenly felt awareness of the rapid and complex question of the obsolescence of knowledge has prompted professional associations (of engineers, doctors, the legal profession, accountants, etc.) to encourage, oblige, or even organise, its members' continuing education, sometimes for a specified number of hours. Professional structural changes are farther-reaching and more rapid however, and accumulating new knowledge is not enough. It must be developed and applied to increasing numbers of associated areas and changing situations, especially by professionals in constant contact with related disciplines.

But adults are seen to constitute a diversified *clientèle* with different needs left unmet by the formal system. Different providers have emerged, each seeking to meet the needs of the many categories of adults concerned.

Developments outside the formal system

In most Member countries, continuing education and continuing professional education have basically developed outside formal secondary and higher educational structures, considered too rigid in their objectives, content, methods and funding arrangements to accommodate a new type of education. As OECD (1977) remarks, "whereas regular schools still often emphasize institutional discipline, adult education promotes social integration within defined groups voluntarily assembled together. Instead of fostering general understanding and indeterminate skills, it fosters specific understanding and specific skills. Its goal is usually single rather than multipurpose. It does not cater to uniform age groups and in general it uses group techniques and encourages a high degree of individualised learning. Finally, it starts from the premise that only adults can change social reality here and now'' (p. 54).

The question of the relationship with the formal education system remains open today, despite the fact that countries have more or less explicitly adopted one or another strategy, ranging from non-intervention by the public authorities to the planned integration of initial and continuing education, exemplified by the Swedish reform of the 1970s.

From the start, adult education has, indeed, been far more than a substitute for formal education. It quickly shed its marginality, although few countries have invested in an overall integrative educational strategy. As early as 1977, OECD identified different development models for adult education, either integrated into the general education system in countries opting for a recurrent education strategy, or treated as a separate and more or less co-ordinated sector in those countries preferring to retain a diversified educational structure.

In addition, twenty years ago, there was already a political, economic, social and cultural need to provide adequate, country-wide adult education in all modern societies. Having established that the different functions of adult education were not interlinked, and that certain populations among the most disadvantaged were benefiting least from education, OECD emphasized the need to reinforce and co-ordinate the range of existing activities while pursuing a positive support policy for priority activities. However, the shortcomings in the relationship between continuing and formal education also stem from conceptual ambiguities about adult and continuing education.

Recurrent Education: Trends and Issues (1975) also suggested that formulating a coherent recurrent education policy could be related to initial education, and to other considerations of public concern such as the labour force, employment and leisure. In the 1980s, the bearing of continuing education on vocational preoccupations gained in importance, whereas initial and continuing education became less important. Now, thinking is turning towards the practical implications of continuing education's growth. The time has now come for higher education to ask ''what is required'' in order for the education system to evolve. As the debates on the length of study and the relationship between general and vocational education show, these issues are still far from being resolved.

Mass continuing education

In 1987, the results of the survey carried out by CERI, *Adults in Higher Education* (OECD, 1987a) drew attention to a sharp divergence in higher education practices with a large-scale social and vocational impact in the Member countries. The survey focused on adults over 25 years of age, enrolled in degree courses in institutions of higher education able to award university or State degrees, certificates and diplomas, and considered their situation, the influence of new information and telecommunications technology (CEC, 1991) and the growing importance of university education and professional education.

The situation of adults

For a variety of reasons, adults are no longer a minority whose studies are short-term and non-degree.[2] Indeed, by the end of the 1980s, because of structural and demographic changes, rising unemployment and the large-scale entry of women into the workforce, adults were coming to constitute one of the main clienteles in higher education. Unfortunately, as is the case with most studies concerning highly mobile innovative areas, virtually no statistical data existed to determine the magnitude of the phenomenon. OECD (1987a) sought to collect information on the essential questions posed by the presence of adults in higher education in order to facilitate a coherent approach to their situation. Despite the particular difficulties involved (lack of information and guidance, difficulties of part-time study, rigid admission procedures, financial problems, etc.), what is clear is the enormous diversity in supply and demand.

As we move into a new decade, adults constitute a heterogeneous group with diversified requirements and advantages to offer to higher education institutions, particularly in terms of a rapprochement between higher education and employment.

Adults in Higher Education (OECD, 1987a) notes that adults' goals and reasons for undertaking study range from personal enrichment to improved career prospects. At one end of the spectrum, a minority of adults are enrolled at a university for an initial degree, and at the other end, a majority are taking one or more short-term courses (OECD, 1982). It is clear that degree and non-degree seekers have different goals. In the United States it is especially clear that many of those in continuing adult education in non-vocational subjects (*e.g.* the liberal arts) have entered these programmes for vocational reasons (US Department of Education, 1985).

These demands are not mutually exclusive, and may overlap. Nor are they directed solely at institutions of formal higher education. Other providers (enterprises, professional associations, etc.) have now been responding to these demands for many years.

The OECD (1987a) pointed out that the ongoing hesitations of higher education institutions in most Member countries must be considered in conjunction with the range of education offered by enterprises, unions, public broadcasting and television corporations, trade associations, chambers of commerce and industry, and a number of commercial firms. Continuing education is co-ordinated in different ways with the traditions of universities and other institutions of higher education, which explains the different relationships between adults seeking continuing education and the higher education institutions providing it. It is noteworthy that between 1980 and 1985, continuing education did not usually figure among the missions of higher education institutions whereas today, there is marked progress.

The emergence of continuing professional education

Since the mid-1980s, continuing professional education has been emerging as a category of continuing education distinct from recurrent education, second-chance opportunities, and adult education. A chapter in *Adults in Higher Education* (OECD, 1987a) was devoted to continuing professional education, already acknowledged as the most vigorously changing and expanding aspect of continuing education.

Higher-level continuing professional education was defined as professional refresher and updating course-work for physicians, lawyers, teachers, civil engineers, or architects, for example, holding higher education degrees. Universities played a very minor role in providing education of this type, predominantly offered by professional associations – especially in professions where continuing education was sometimes obligatory – chambers of commerce and industry, and specialised institutions outside the higher education system. Together with private organisations, these associations offered an increasing range of continuing professional education courses. The growth of this movement led a number of professional associations to propose new strategies of continuing professional education in partnership with higher education which, as we will see, extended its traditional mission.

Adults in Higher Education raised the issue of the specific role of the universities in responding to the demands for continuing professional education for highly-qualified personnel, given that no other type of institution possessed either the human or material resources, or the necessary scientific and technological knowledge. Since the philosophical shift in the early 1980s, higher education has been assigning ever greater importance to continuing education, which now ranks alongside its two traditional missions of providing initial higher education of young people, and research. Yet, in terms of quantity and diversity, these institutions cannot satisfy the demand for adult education, particularly for the rapidly growing continuing professional education of highly-qualified personnel. This is an area in which companies and professional associations have always played a major role, and where new providers are appearing on the scene. It is also widely accepted that the increasing numbers of higher education graduates have to refresh and update their knowledge in response to scientific and technical advances, changes in relevant laws and regulations (the Single European Market of 1993), structural changes, etc. All these factors create a dynamic climate favouring rapid growth in demand, and, it is to be hoped, a growing response from higher education.

Diversified higher education

Since the 1960s, higher education in all the OECD countries has grown massively and opened up. The student population has changed along with changed social, economic and cultural expectations of higher education. The traditional roles and missions of university and non-university higher education have thus been affected.

The coexistence in higher education of different age groups of students has made governments aware of the need to diversify institutions. This is a major element in the development of higher education policies; since the 1960s, institutions performing new functions have been set up, and in their forefront are those providing short, additional courses which complement traditional university missions (OECD, 1987*b*).

Over the last twenty years, non-university higher education institutions have developed considerably, and have been legitimated within the national systems. This growth

(OECD, 1991b) is characterised by greater vocational orientation, more applied research, vigorous relations with industry and answerability to the community and the region.

Considerable clarification will be needed to define the success of these institutions (enrolments, course quality and relevance to employers and individuals, first job salary levels, unemployment rates, etc.) The option has earned a special image as closer to employment by creating university-level occupational education attuned to economic and social developments of the Member countries. On the one hand, access to higher education has been opened up to "non-traditional" groups, and on the other, new concepts and programme organisation have helped endow this form of education with a positive image for students and employers alike.

Non-university institutions have basically endeavoured to respond to the needs of young persons with qualifications different from those required for university entrance. Adult participation has been less widely encouraged, even though, in some countries like the United States, it is on the increase because of the interest in continuing occupational education. Non-university education is a natural choice for adults because it is more inclined to cater to their needs and better prepared to supply the services required.

If, during the 1980s, the "group" of adults interested in higher education also diversified, the university responded slowly and basically in piecemeal fashion. "Clienteles" associated themselves with specific, discrete elements of the university, generally outside the traditional academic framework. Continuing education in response to new demands from non-traditional, non-degree seekers failed to make much impression on the university image.

More recently, adults' demands for continuing education have been more or less vigorous, depending on the national, social and cultural contexts. In Canada, for instance, the public targeted by continuing professional education in higher education institutions is enormous and includes primary and secondary-school teachers, managers, nurses, accountants, managerial staff, engineers, adult instructors, lawyers, government administrators, social workers and bank employees. The choice is the responsibility of the individual in the education process. Higher education institutions have broadened the range of their partnerships, and a profound transformation is taking place in the concept of higher education and in its relationship with the economic, social and cultural environment.

These new demands for continuing education differ from those of traditional students enrolling in a homogeneous process of initial higher education offered within a single structure. Continuing professional education responds to the demands of diversified clienteles with a variety of educational needs, institutional arrangements, certification requirements, financial resources, etc. Moreover, on theoretical grounds, the language used in initial and higher education has created barriers between the latter and employment which continuing education could help to overcome. No single type of provider, however, can respond to diverse demands, whatever the multiplicity of its institutions and its new forms of organisation and teaching, *e.g.* distance education and part-time studies. Some types of education are better handled by companies, training enterprises, professional associations. Redefining higher education's responsibilities requires paying close attention to selecting the direction for developing continuing professional education.

Alternatives to Universities (OECD, 1991*b*) points out that the rapprochement between university education and non-university education, which share common values, is likely to continue in future years. Present trends will ineluctably change the balance of the higher education, however, which must maintain quality but also reconcile it with different pedagogy, continue to do cutting edge research in an internationalising context, and respond to pressing external demands for a highly accessible system. Future economic and social prospects of society depend on this.

The emergence of other educational sectors

Following the development of education outside the formal sector, a commercial sector or "third sector", "private training sector" or "training industry", has emerged in the last few years.

The commercial sector is having an important and growing influence on the continuing professional education market, and consequently on the position, roles, and functions of institutions of higher education. As OECD (1991*b*) points out in a study concerned with initial higher education, "This sector, as yet ill-defined, consists of a wide range of programmes, predominantly privately organised and financed either by profit-making educational institutions charging substantial fees (*e.g.* proprietary schools in the United States) or by firms. Most often they are of short duration and narrowly vocational. Joint public/private schemes are also developing rapidly. In some countries this trend is being encouraged and/or supported by public authorities under the umbrella of different ministries (p. 72)".

But in the context of continuing professional education, the development of the private training sector has been at least as rapid and widespread, if not more so. This upsurge coexists with decelerated growth in the university and non-university sector in many Member countries – which itself points to a vacuum in training provision. Compensating for post-secondary education is felt in initial education and, to a greater extent, in continuing professional education, which lacks such highly structured provision.

Market forces are therefore playing a more powerful role in continuing professional education where the intervention of public authorities is comparatively limited. Non-university education is feeling the pressure of the "commercial sector" more vigorously, because its short and highly occupational courses sometimes closely approximate non-university offerings. In this sense, competition between the commercial sector and non-university education is far greater than that between the commercial sector and the universities because the non-university sector can most easily adopt market strategies and compete directly with the commercial sector. Universities are generally less ready to move in this direction; they offer products and services which differ quite substantially from those of the commercial sector, and are more shielded from the effects of this competition.

Relations with the economic environment

The evolution of the relationship between higher education institutions and their economic environment is visible in initial training, research, and in the increasing scope of activities connected with continuing professional education. The 1980s were characterised by a marked reduction in public-sector recruitment from educational establishments, and by the opening-up of new opportunities in industry (Esnault, 1990; OECD, 1993). By contrast with previous decades, the private sector is now the chief provider of job opportunities for university graduates. This shift is symptomatic of a profound change in the relationship between higher education and employment (Esnault, 1990). Continuing professional education has often been the site where these concerns meet. The dialogue begun some years ago between higher education and the labour market has enabled those responsible for the economy and industry better to know and understand the "products" of higher education, and those responsible for higher education to respond with greater awareness and/or a greater spirit of accommodation to economic needs, expectations and demands.

In 1984, an OECD report, noted the importance which public authorities gave to the creation of non-formal networks, and to improved organisation of the links considered essential for technology transfers. This, as has been noted in several country contributions (Germany, Austria), is also one way of promoting the development of continuing education within higher education institutions.

In 1990, universities have far broader relationships with business than with industry. The work of the Committee for scientific and technological policy (OECD, 1989*b*) shows that we are witnessing:

a) A reinforcement of relationships, as the low percentage of industry-funded university research attests, symptomatic of an externalisation of research activities by firms.

b) A rapprochement between basic and applied research, evident in the reduced transfer time for expertise and technological know-how (*cf.* biotechnologies, electronics).

Collaboration between universities and enterprises has become a reality with its own dynamic potential. The work carried out by the Group on Scientific and University Research has led to the formulation of a typology of relations distinguishing various forms of collaboration: research and training now figure as separate entities (OECD, 1989*c*). While education or training are not the central purpose of such work, the study conducted over the past five years has pin-pointed the rapid growth in training and its improved adaptation to company needs. There is more collaboration in education (exchange of personnel), continuing education, and the formulation of training programmes in advanced technologies (the CIFRE programme in France).

Despite the absence of quantitative proof, enterprises appear to be quickly learning to use university potential, especially basic research and very advanced education or training. Conversely, universities, under the burden of increasing budgetary constraints, have awakened to the need for relations with the business world, and have more clearly defined their objectives in this area. Notwithstanding obstacles and the intrinsic difficulties, collaboration is growing rapidly and relationships have now been formalised and have become a priority objective in the scientific and technological policies of many Member countries.

In addition, it is now accepted that the economic environment benefits from the establishment of higher education institutions, particularly at regional level. The Scandinavian countries, Canada, France, Japan, the Netherlands, the United States, and others make use of higher education institutions to promote the economic, social and cultural welfare of geographically remote regions, of rural areas and of regions undergoing economic restructuring (OECD, 1992, 1989c).

Closing remarks

There is at present an unquestionable diversity of demand for continuing education, and a rather unstructured response by providers (Colardyn, 1990). Every part of the adult population generates its own specific requirements to be met by higher education institutions, or by the other providers. These new clients seek:

a) publicly accessible education including remedial courses, community college courses in the United States or the "courses for elders" in France;
b) further initial education courses including preparatory courses for initial admission to institutions of higher education (United Kingdom, France, Germany);
c) "Master's" courses generally of two years' duration, including any form of advanced education or post-graduate training. Several countries mention that this type of training is growing very rapidly and extensively, organised either by the university sector (Spain, the United States, France), or by enterprises (Italy);
d) continuing professional education aimed at qualified personnel, with or without initial higher education but with extended occupational experience. With their employer's agreement, they pursue general or specialised continuing education connected with their current jobs, or with possibilities of redeployment or promotion;
e) refresher courses for teachers, traditionally offered in institutions of higher education. Teachers are not included in the scope of this project.

Increased offerings, diversification, emergence of new providers all point to the growth and diversification of continuing education demands, despite the paucity of figures to evaluate the phenomenon directly (see Annex 1) or predict its future course. Higher education is attempting to cope with the many facets of the demand and other providers now in the market are also offering more or less suitable means for satisfying the need. The market tends to favour competition which is not yet largely or fully established. Higher education needs policy directives to overcome its hesitancy or difficulties in taking up this challenge.

Notes

1. *Recurrent Education* (OECD, 1975): "It argues not for new educational objectives but basically an alternative of educational opportunity, where the present system is gradually transformed so that it no longer provides education in one stretch during the individual's youth, but over his whole lifetime and in alternation with other activities and in particular with work (p. 7)".
   Learning opportunities for Adults (OECD, 1977): "(...) adult education refers to any learning activity or programme deliberately designed to satisfy any learning need or interest that may be experienced at any stage in his or her life by a person who is over the statutory school-leaving age and whose principal activity is no longer in education (p. 7)".
2. After the Second World War, the United States, for example, introduced special measures (the GI Bill) to enable adults (ex-service personnel) to enter higher education. This legislation opened up higher education in an extraordinary way, and led to innovations affecting the recognition and transfer of non-academic competences. Although the same philosophy did not generate direct equivalents in other countries, public authorities frequently initiated measures to assist adults in gaining access to continuing education and higher education in general.

Chapter II

Segmentation of Continuing Professional Education

Some countries (Sweden, France, Italy, the Netherlands) are attempting to treat the development of higher education and continuing education globally. Others, for various reasons, have opted for a *laissez-faire* policy. A third category, where developments are fairly recent, have not fully grasped the magnitude of the phenomenon. There is a clear need to know what is happening for all concerned. This chapter considers continuing professional education for highly-qualified personnel particularly in order to clarify the specificities of the responses made by institutions of higher education.

The major challenge for institutions of higher education is to define their place and their role in the continuing professional education market although little information exists to assess this. An initial attempt at clarification will therefore be based on a close examination of the education and training provided by institutions of higher education and other providers.

A number of theoretical and incomplete criteria reflect the complexity of a situation in which the segments overlap. An initial analysis suggests that training is offered according to the following criteria: providers; financing; educational level; discipline; occupation.

Defining the providers

Institutional providers in the training market is a "powerful" criterion, because it can give a direct idea of different market shares. All participating countries in this project recognise this segmentation although there is no unique operating model. The positions and roles of the various providers have to be understood within their particular national contexts and these can contrast sharply. Market shares can be defined in terms of numbers of individuals trained, numbers of hours of training or the amount of funds concerned. Using one or another of these benchmarks can convey a rather different, or even divergent, picture of the extent to which these providers are involved in the training market.

Each provider in the continuing professional education market possesses particular advantages. Higher education institutions have, as yet little used, multidisciplinary and up-to-date scientific facilities. Enterprises are current on practical problems, and can offer possible short-term solutions. Professional associations have unparalleled access to examples of the "best practice" and to a fund of occupational expertise and knowledge. Profit-making agencies are able to adapt quickly to, and exploit, market opportunities, and are not bound by medium- or long-term education or training policies.

Enterprises: internal markets and human resource management

Training and, in some countries, training departments, are becoming increasingly important in companies. Large corporations are often highly active. Small- and medium-sized enterprises have difficulties taking their place in the further training and continuing education "networks" because of budget and timing constraints (organisation of work, problem of replacing personnel undergoing training, funding problems). Countries with heavy business commitment to the continuing professional education of highly-qualified personnel include Japan, the United States and France. By contrast, firms in the United Kingdom and Canada have a limited traditional commitment to in-house continuing education of their personnel (Canada, 1987, 1989).

An example of under-developed internal training

Canada stands out as an interesting example of a country with a weak tradition of in-house training. In essence, individuals are primarily responsible for sustaining and developing their skills and competences, although encouragement and even funding may be provided by the federal or the provincial authorities. Some of the largest private associations, such as the Conference Board of Canada and the Canadian Manufacturers Association, are calling upon enterprises to play a greater role in continuing education particularly because of the frequent criticisms made of the quality and relevance of the formal education system. Some large corporations, or some industrial sectors, have set up non-profit education and training centres. The Petroleum Industry Training Service, for example, offers education and training courses for newcomers and established workers in the oil industry. Noteworthy as well is the growing influence of a forum where the heads of large corporations meet university presidents to discuss the possibilities for collaboration and partnerships between industry and higher education (the Corporate Higher Education Forum).

A national survey on the state of continuing professional education for Canadian engineers (Heinke and Weihs, 1990) indicates that the companies questioned claimed to be actively supporting continuing education, although they were unable to estimate how many engineers were currently involved. Enterprises dominate the continuing education of engineers by virtue of the funding and the physical facilities (documentation centres, computer facilities) which they make available. The authors also mention another recent survey carried out by telephoning thirty-three, mostly large, companies. The results underline the significance of the funding provided by employers for education and training courses linked to career prospects of individuals *within the company,* and also noted that most internal education and training facilities target management. Two of the companies contacted had introduced "certificates of completion of internal education and training", which were placed on the individual's file and considered in performance evaluation.

The growth of internal training

In general, however, enterprises in most other Member countries, except Canada, are increasingly involved in continuing education. Initially, continuing professional education of highly-qualified personnel was often externalised. In recent years, a marked tendency favouring internal education and training, including education and training outside of working hours has emerged (Norway, France, Switzerland) for several reasons: a growing opinion that the training of managerial staff is, in the main, the company's responsibility, and that external training can only provide a desirable and necessary complement; and a real concern to provide "custom-made" education and training, combining external and internal expertise and allowing overall supervision of the educational process as an element in the individual's career development.

In Austria, surveys point to the growing involvement of enterprises in the continuing education of all personnel categories. In 1981, for instance, Austrian companies were spending about AS 1 000 per employee per annum for training. By 1986, the expenditure rose to an estimated AS 2 800 per employee per annum. Internal continuing education provision generally compensates for some regional disparities in the public continuing education system. Companies also co-operate with other providers. In all cases, corporate strategies continue to seek custom-made training, even if this means increasing internal provision or relying more heavily on external providers.

In the United States, employers' total outlay for education and training purposes may represent between $32 to $100 billion, or as much as three-quarters of the annual national expenditure on education by educational institutions. Unfortunately, no data exist to enable us to determine the percentage of this amount specifically allocated to the continuing professional education of highly-qualified personnel.

Switzerland provides a very complete picture of the expansion, which it emphasizes, of the internal training market in the banking sector, characterised by a growing need for skilled personnel. Between 1983 and 1986, its staff increased by approximately 15 per cent and the percentage of personnel with a higher education level more than doubled. The 1980 survey showed that only a quarter of managerial staff had a higher education level, however, and it is therefore clear that only internal training can enable the banking sector to train the other three-quarters. Over the years, a number of internal training facilities have been instituted, including basic vocational training, higher or university-level occupational education, and training for managerial staff. Basic vocational training continues today to be the main access route into the banking business. Higher or university-level occupational education usually follows an apprenticeship, and assumes that the student already has several years of professional experience. Professional associations are responsible for the examinations to which this training leads.

Young university graduates are very sought-after recruits, and banks attract them with various training schemes to banking careers in marketing, finance, accounts, etc. These 6- to 18-month training periods may be rounded off by a 2-day "academic assessment" designed to gauge team spirit, articulateness, will, problem-solving capacity and working technique. The education and training of managerial staff is designed not merely to prepare the "next generation", but also to reinforce and enhance managerial qualities and the ability to manage staff. Corporate strategies make the links between internal training policies, career management and the overriding need for custom-made training evident. For instance, the Wolsberg training centre of the Union of Swiss Banks offers education and training programmes that run parallel to career development (Table 1). It exemplifies the co-ordination between continuing education policy and human resource management: early marshalling of knowledge, preparation for senior management positions, training selected members of management teams, etc. The seminars proposed by Crédit Suisse involve continuing education in teams. Groups work together and participate in a single course mixing all hierarchical levels. Its main advantage appears to lie in the easier transfer of knowledge, which is not restricted to the trainees, but spreads throughout the working "cell".

The concern for knowledge transfer, and the practice of team education and training also characterise leading-edge Norwegian enterprises (in the computer sector). As is often the case with fairly highly developed training and human resource management policies, every candidate for a managerial position is obliged to pass through the company's assessment centre.

Partial externalisation of training

Several country contributions have referred to a recent trend of partially externalising continuing professional education. In France, a survey done by the *Centre d'Etudes et de Recherches sur les Qualifications* (research and study centre on qualifications – CEREQ) has shown that the intensity of continuing education effort on all employees,

Table 1. **Switzerland: market for internal continuing education and career development**

- Introductory seminar (trainees aged 24-28)
  16-week course, divided into three periods over two years, intended for candidates for senior management positions (section heads)
- Basic training seminar (trainees aged 30-40)
  12-week course, spread over a 3-year period, intended for candidates for senior management positions (section heads)
- Continuing education seminar (trainees aged 40-50)
  2-week course, intended for future members of management (main section, department, and branch managers)
- Senior training seminar I (trainees aged 35-65)
  1-week course for all members of management
- Senior training seminar II (trainees aged 35-65)
  1-week course in company management (for selected members of management)
- Senior training course III (trainees aged 35-65)
  2- to 3-day course for supervisory organs (board of directors, and supervisory board)

Source: Swiss contribution, 1990.

and not just the highly-skilled, and internalisation of education and training (Géhin, 1989) are directly proportional. Between 1973 and 1985, the internal training expenditure of many industrial sectors was reduced by a factor of 2 or 3, or even more. Across the whole range of business activities, expenditures for internal training dropped from 25 to 17.8 per cent of total outlay. There are several possible explanations:

a) During the 1970s, firms were trying to free themselves from the previous, weighty education and training structures. This resulted in the closure of internal training centres and in externalisation.

b) Technological and organisational changes are leading towards a more narrowly defined, specialised knowledge requiring expertise which does not always exist within the enterprise. The need to import such expertise favours the process of externalisation.

c) The relationship between firms and outside training providers has been strengthened.

Externalisation policies vary by occupational sector; there are three groups in France. One is made up of sectors which undertake intense, in-house training and continuing education (electricity, gas and water, transport, oil, insurance, vehicle manufacture); a second undertakes fairly large-scale training, in which recourse to external facilities has grown greatly (electrical engineering, electronics, aircraft, shipbuilding, armaments, iron and steel, basic chemicals and chemicals-related, and pharmaceutics). A third group engages in a low level of further training and continuing professional education, and is not committing itself further. There is considerable, though diminishing, recourse to external facilities (trade sector, consumer goods industries, the agro-food sector and mechanical engineering). A substitution process is underway here to the detriment of training facilities and to the benefit of the Fund for Continuing Training introduced by the 1971 legislation, to which employers contribute a percentage of their payroll.

In the United Kingdom, for different reasons, the weak tradition of in-company further training and continuing education has led employers to turn to the outside training market rather than develop internal facilities. The United Kingdom contribution indicates that, nationally, enterprises are not very satisfied with the education and provision offered by higher education institutions, although local collaboration and partnerships are beginning, and dialogue is gaining ground.

In Italy recently, continuing education has been partly externalised. Historically, some large corporations (Olivetti and Fiat) created the first private education and training institutes for managerial staff around the 1950s, along the American model. These experiments were long disregarded by universities wishing to safeguard their academic traditions. The 1970s saw the beginnings of change, and a greater readiness for co-operation between the universities and the business world (Boccini University, Masters at Milan Polytechnic) which turned to the universities, as they realised that on-the-job training was too slow and too specific to the level of qualifications at issue here. But universities are neither able nor willing single-handedly to meet by themselves the needs for new skills and competences, which are often too far removed from academic traditions.

The coexistence of internal and partially external continuing education is becoming the hallmark of corporate training strategy. But the criteria by which strategic choices are made are complex. In the German chemical industry, for instance, the continuing education of engineers is organised internally, and calls upon the resources of higher education institutions. In sectors like mechanical engineering, building and civil engineering, internal continuing education is less widespread and non-company institutions (professional associations, chambers of commerce) provide for-fee continuing education.

Partial externalisation sometimes results from a consensual approach aimed at effort-sharing, as the example of the Netherlands illustrates. There, attempts are being made to set up a system based on negotiation between the public authorities and the social partners. In 1989, for example, two-thirds of the joint agreements included provisions for training (covering 80 per cent of the employees affected by the collective bargaining). This applies, for instance, to the banking sector, which offers career-linked rather than functional or job-necessitated education and training opportunities. In the metal-working sector, the social partners have agreed that a sum of up to 0.6 per cent of wages should be used to promote further training and continuing education activities.

Most of these negotiations relate to secondary-level further training. However, employers stress the need to reinforce initial higher education with short-term continuing professional education of "applied post-graduate" type, sometimes referred to as "Masters", in which case they commit themselves to funding the continuing education of managerial staff, even if it is provided by institutions outside the company. Course content remains very closely linked to occupational concerns (accounting, taxation, personnel control and management, languages, etc.), and to interdisciplinary issues concerning, for instance, the environment. The contribution emphasizes that if training and corporate requirements are to be co-ordinated, there must be increased collaboration between the universities, companies and occupational sectors, and education and training must be adjusted, improved and better linked with the world of work.

Japan provides a very interesting example of externalisation. Against a backdrop of obsolescence of knowledge, the changing role of graduates in corporate life, and the erosion of the "lifelong employment" principle, the future of internal continuing education has broad effects. In-company training is no longer adequate except in some large leading-edge corporations. Thoughts are turning to external training provisions because of factors common to all Member countries: technological and knowledge advances, increasingly wide gaps between initially acquired expertise (initial education) and job requirements. In addition, more accessible higher education has altered the mechanisms of career management, a trend which is evident among highly-qualified personnel in mid-career. Lastly, and this is a feature peculiar to the Japanese situation, there is an increase in mobility, especially among young graduates, due to restructuring processes, the lack of certain categories of highly-qualified personnel, and internationalisation.

The effectiveness and relevance of "induction training", accompanied by on-the-job training and redeployment, are no longer sufficient to meet education and training requirements which are more individualised and less closely related to immediate functions: external continuing education becomes a necessary complement and reflects the difference between corporate and individual needs. The beginnings of this new demand

Table 2. **Japan: predicted needs for and actual role of future off-the-job training**
In percentage

Predicted needs	
Needs and actual role will increase	47.9
Needs will increase but actual role will not	35.5
Neither needs nor actual role will increase	16.6

Note: Sample survey of 2 363 business firms with 30 employees or more.
Source: Ministry of Labour, "Report of the Survey on Co-operative Education and Training", 1986.

are already apparent in the current success of correspondence and self-development courses. Surveys show that the Japanese clearly perceive this growing need (Table 2). External training is not necessarily funded by the company, which means that for individuals, career planning is at a turning point. For companies, a change is taking place in human resource management, and an external labour market could emerge as a concomitant of this development of the off-the-job market for continuing education.

Some employers (Switzerland) have adopted a very sharply defined position on the subsidiary role of State aids, refusing the State's right to regulate or promote continuing education measures within companies (Swiss authorities, 1989). Thus, recourse to "private companies", or, as is mentioned in the survey carried out by the Austrian authorities, to university consultants for custom-made in-house training are aspects of partial externalisation integrated into the internal market for the continuing professional education of highly-qualified personnel.

Professional associations

Professional associations have traditionally been very prominent in the initial and continuing education of their members by providing speciality training and broader social understanding. They are increasingly emphasizing their professional education policies with regard to their members. Membership procedures vary by country, which explains the differing roles which these associations play in initial and continuing education. In some countries (the United States, the United Kingdom, Germany, Canada, Denmark), they are an important part of the life of a professional community, in others (Norway, the former Yugoslavia) their essential role is to be the main transmission channel between professionals and higher education institutions; sometimes, their role is practically non-existent (the Netherlands).

Professional associations have become more aware of, and have changed their attitudes towards, continuing professional education as demand has grown and diversified. They generally offer relatively little continuing education themselves. In this respect, the Canadian example of the professional associations of engineers who want to improve their members' career prospects and are thus stepping up education and training is interesting. There is every likelihood of increased continuing professional education of engineers, even though there is no obligation to do so.

When professional associations do directly organise continuing education, it tends to be concerned with ethics and professional conduct in new situations. More generally, they prefer to recognise programmes supplied by other providers and so are rather receptive to the idea of greater activity on the part of the public authorities in favour of outside firms and intersectoral training open to all (Swiss authorities, 1989). They frequently collaborate with higher education institutions: for instance, through the Canadian Engineering Accreditation Board, the Canadian Council of Professional Engineers recognises programmes put forward by higher education institutions. The Canadian Institute of Chartered Accountants follows the same procedure.

For salaried engineers, employers offer a major incentive for participation in continuing education activities. Independent engineers are motivated by the market, to remain competitive. The chief obstacles to participation (Table 3) are workload (53 per cent), other personal activities (34 per cent), and schedule conflicts (27 per cent). Over the previous six months, however, most of the professionals questioned[1] have not taken part in any continuing education activity, although 37 per cent did participate in non-degree/diploma courses. Overall, the most appealing areas of education and training for the engineers questioned are management and information technology.

In many industrial sectors, advisory committees have been set up to handle the particular needs of professional staff. Different ways of recording acquired knowledge and experience are currently being tried out by professional associations who: *a)* recognise units of continuing education; *b)* create certificates; *c)* establish and manage a databank on engineers who have completed qualified formal education activities.

Informal or on-the-job training (reading professional journals, discussions with colleagues) no longer suffices as a substitute for further training for many professionals; it is too slow, too incomplete and too unreliable, according to professional associations. Seminars, conferences and technical journals arranged and edited by technical societies constitute a large share of the non-formal further training available to engineers. Canadian professional associations stress that prior relations between universities and corpora-

Table 3. **Canada: reasons given by engineers for failing to participate in continuing education activity**

In percentage

1.	Workload	53
2.	Other personal activities	34
3.	Conflict of schedule	27
4.	Distance	20
5.	Duration of activity	14
6.	Costs	13

Source: Canadian contribution, 1991.

tions are conducive to collaboration in continuing professional education. Analyses by OECD's Committee for Scientific and Technological Policy (OECD, 1989*b*) concur. Joint research and development activities create education and training initially linked to current basic or applied research, and subsequently gaining more autonomy (seminars, workshops, training sessions).

In the United States, professional regulations governing each profession means that the content, quality and quantity of continuing professional education fall to the professions themselves. This practice results in enormous numbers of standards reflecting the requirements of each professional organisation in each state. Furthermore, professional associations are seeking the back-up of government regulations in a growing number of cases. Government, para-statal, and private agencies all intervene in formulating educational norms to meet the requirements of professional associations. Regulations often spring from public safety and security issues, and are nationally and locally rooted in cases of incompetence and fraud which can be found in any profession. Strict rulings governing professional entry requirements and the use of continuing professional education counter these problems and increase the social and economic appeal of the profession. This is why continuing training is more often a condition for license renewal (Table 4).

In the United Kingdom, professional associations lay down training standards and objectives, and help their members determine their continuing professional education

Table 4. **United States: growth of state-mandated continuing professional education, 1979-89**

Profession	Number of states (50) mandating	
	As of 1979	As of 1989
Accounting	28	48
Real Estate	11	33
Law	8	33
Social work	10	26
Nursing home administration	42	45
Psychology (clinical)	7	19
Nursing (registered)	10	11
Nursing (licensed practical)	8	12
Physical therapy	3	10
Dentistry	9	14
Optometry	45	47
Pharmacy	21	42
Medicine	20	22
Veterinary medicine	19	28
Architecture	1	1
Engineering (professional)	1	1

Source: Louis Phillips, "Mandatory Continuing Education Update", *Newsletter,* p. 1, Summer 1989, Louis Phillips and Associates, Athens, GA.

needs. Many associations have devised their own continuing professional education policy, and the Engineering Council has without doubt played an important pilot role in recent years. Recent surveys confirm the growing commitment of these associations regarding continuing professional education, and various of their actions indicate the emergence of a continuing professional education strategy (Vaughn and Squires, 1990). Although this commitment to continuing education should not be overstated, it does take various forms, ranging from the production of material for distance education to the establishment of partnerships, particularly with higher education institutions.

In Denmark, three main professional associations provide continuing professional education:

a) the Union of Danish PhDs, Masters of Arts and Masters of Science (MA group);
b) the Danish Lawyers' and Economists' Association (SSC group);
c) the Society of Engineers of Denmark (TEK group).

Each of these associations covers a group of disciplines (Table 5). The MA has recently made a major breakthrough into the private sector. It has also set up continuing education and in 1989 accounted for 3 per cent of the market "managed" by professional associations. It provides continuing education that focuses on short-term courses, lasting 2-3 days, and laying equal emphasis on occupational training and personal development (Table 6). Clearly, this market is dominated by the Society of Engineers, which provides 76 per cent of all continuing education offered by professional associations, followed by the Lawyers' and Economists' Association (SSC group). The Society of Engineers is by far the most heavily committed to long-term continuing education.

In Germany, for professions like physicians and lawyers, professional associations are essentially responsible for continuing education which is sometimes compulsory (medicine).

In Norway, professional associations act as intermediaries between individuals and providers in the training market (supplying information and guidance services), and

Table 5. **Denmark: six main groups for which the Danish Federation of Professional Associations has the right to conduct collective negotiations, 1987**

1. Masters of arts and science (MA), approximately 24 000 members
2. Graduates in social sciences (SSC) approximately 20 000 members
3. Graduates in technical sciences (TEK), approximately 24 000 members
4. Graduates in medical sciences (MED), approximately 22 000 members
5. Graduates in agricultural and veterinary sciences (AG-VE), approximately 6 000 members
6. Graduates educated in the military forces (FAC), approximately 2 500 members

Note: Together, the six groups count approximately 100 000 university graduates engaged in active employment. To this figure should be added 6 500 persons who were unemployed at the time of counting, and 26 000 engineers graduated from technical schools.
Source: Danish contribution, 1991.

Table 6. **Denmark: continuing professional education provided by the further training institute for professional associations, 1989***

Days	Professional specialisation	Personal development	Management
One day	MA[a]: 69 (8%) SSC[b]: 834 (15%) TEK[c]: 1 847 (10%)	MA: – SSC: – TEK: 357 (1%)	MA: 17 (2%) SSC: – TEK: 183 (1%)
2-3 days	MA: 401 (48%) SSC: 3 888 (74%) TEK: 4 339 (22%)	MA: 352 (42%) SSC: 283 (5%) TEK: 4 185 (21%)	MA: – SSC: 129 (2%) TEK: 285 (1%)
Longer courses	MA: – SSC: 220 (4%) TEK: 923 (5%)	MA: – SSC: – TEK: 3 033 (15%)	MA: – SSC: – TEK: 5 282 (26%)
Totals	MA: 839 SSC: 5 354 TEK: 20 434		

* The activity is indicated for each type of course by number of days x number of participants.
a) MA – Union of Danish PhDs, Masters of Arts and Masters of Science.
b) SSC – Danish Lawyers' and Economists' Association.
c) TEK – Society of Engineers of Denmark.
Source: Danish contribution, 1991.

constitute the main channel of communication through which universities and colleges are notified of required professional skills or competences. Institutions of higher education are chiefly involved in long-term courses and they issue certificates which guarantee quality; professional associations offer short courses and seminars. Among a number of interesting experiments that might be mentioned are the Professional Development Certificates (PDC), organised on the basis of modules, and the Group Studies in Management and Administration (GILA), aimed at engineers in managerial positions.

In the former Yugoslavia, associations are responsible for education and training and play an important part in organising courses, seminars, conferences and summer schools for their members. They regularly co-operate with universities, and the country contribution notes that, while the public authorities have long restricted the associations' role, there is a trend towards enlarging their mission (OECD, 1990c).

In the Netherlands, professional associations could quickly come to play a significant role in continuing education, evidenced by the activities of the Netherlands Institute for the Banking and Security Sector (NIBE). Similarly, the Royal Institute of Engineers and the Netherlands Engineers' Association are endeavouring to harmonize the interests of employers, professional staff and education, by using continuing professional education as the basis for discussion.

In conclusion, national professional associations have different commitments to their members' initial and continuing education. The general trend is one of a growing presence, and a wish to institute continuing professional education policies, in collaboration with higher education institutions, if possible.

The commercial sector: attempting a definition

The classification suggested by the Secretariat is an approximation to reality in the various Member countries. Slight variations occur, particularly in the overlap between the commercial sector and what countries define as the "private training sector", or agencies which are not within the public realm. It is, on the whole, fairly recent and is not well known.

This heading covers commercial training enterprises and for-profit training associations but does not include the entire private sector which in most countries encompasses non-profit associations, chambers of commerce, and other education or training agencies with educational, and not commercial aims. In recent years, the private training industry has grown considerably. Education and training enterprises, often closely linked to firms or professional associations, provide courses that are very closely tailored to the needs of the labour market, but are not always homogeneous nor is their quality guaranteed.

The commercial sector is well established in the economic fabric and reported to be growing very rapidly in France, Norway, Sweden, the United Kingdom and the United States. It focuses chiefly on short-term courses and has the reputation of providing excellent training in areas like management, which do not call for initial heavy material investments. Training relating to specific expertise provided in particular professions is generally less well regarded. In the United Kingdom, there are about 1 450 institutions of the "private training enterprise" type, and an estimated one to two hundred play an appreciable role in the continuing professional education market.

Expertise level and quality of service, rather than cost, determine competition between enterprises. Recently, the most reputable training enterprises have been seeking links with institutions of higher education so that both institutions would provide education and training or agreements would allow access to the higher education institutions.

Information in countries such as the United States, the United Kingdom, Sweden, Norway, Italy, France, the Netherlands and Finland, although scarce, stresses the growth of this sector in the 1980s. A number of trends are apparent:

a) internationalisation, especially noticeable in the "management" sector: a growing number of contacts between equivalent training enterprises in other countries;

b) following very rapid growth until 1988/89, some countries, like Norway, experienced a sharp drop in enrolments (by about 30 per cent) and a rapidly increasing participation in custom-made courses (up by 10 per cent);

c) activities are not regulated, and do not share the same social criteria as those governing the public sector (equity, second chance);

d) there is an evident trend towards custom-made courses and in-house training;

e) in general, technical courses are offered only in information technology. Sales and services courses are major fields for them, especially in connection with their consulting business. Management training is provided but there is increased competition from higher education institutions.

In the Netherlands, for instance, training enterprises in the commercial sector usually offer short-term courses to the employed, whereas private schools provide long- and short-term initial and continuing education for part-time or full-time students.

In Norway, the commercial sector includes: enterprises whose sole product is training; training enterprises within consultancy firms; equipment sellers who include training in the sales package; private schools funded by trade organisations (employers); private schools organised as "limited companies"; private schools organised as non-profit associations.

In France, the commercial sector, whose spectacular growth has been noted (CEREQ, 1988), includes: specialised and often small educational and training companies; enterprises in which continuing education is not the main concern such as companies engaged in consultancy work, management, marketing, publishing or advertising; large corporations manufacturing capital equipment (electronic and computer systems, machine-tools). An estimated 40 per cent of total funding is channelled through "enterprises" in this sector, as compared with around 30 per cent in 1980.

The United States contribution draws attention to the significance of providers outside the (public and private) education systems, and notes the activity of thousands of private consultancy firms and consultants. The American Management Association survey of 1982 arrived at a figure of 7 500 contracts with individuals for setting up 100 000 courses and seminars.

In Italy, private-sector continuing education emerged and flourished as a "compensation" for the shortfall in the continuing professional education offered by formal higher education. To encourage its development, the Italian system leaves every door open. The most widespread and highly developed legal mechanism is the consortium, in which private industry represents over 70 per cent of the sponsorship. Private profit-making training enterprises – the "third sector" – account for 43 per cent of the training organisations in the private system and 11.5 per cent of the total – public and private systems (Table 7). 89.5 per cent of the public-sector education system depend on the public authorities and non-profit associations, while government-funded private companies represent a mere 2 per cent of training organisations.

In Canada, this sector has grown rapidly due to policy and funding changes following the realisation that these training organisations (or enterprises) are more flexible and responsive to targeted objectives. In recent years, this trend has been such that the government is considering changing the legislation relating to private and especially commercial institutions. There are about 900 profit-making "private schools" active in business, administration and management, engineering sciences, applied sciences and technology. Teaching staff in the formal sector are making it clear that the commercial sector is winning an increasing share of the continuing education market, to the detriment

Table 7. **Italy: higher continuing professional education: institutional framework of education centres**

	Private[a] system		Public[a] system	
	n.	%	n.	%
Local public authorities	29	13.1	193	26.1
Other public authorities	26	11.7	49	7.1
Non-recognised association	27	12.2	211	28.5
Recognised association	15	6.8	206	27.8
Foundation	4	1.8	6	0.8
Commercial companies	95	43.0	16	2.1
Other private organisations	1	0.5	1	0.1
Consortium of public authorities	2	0.9	22	3.0
Consortium of firms	7	3.2	13	1.7
Mixed consortium	15	6.8	6	0.8
Consortium of associations	–	–	7	0.9
Other kinds of organisations	–	–	9	1.1
Total	221	100.0	739	100.0

a) These figures concern 739 centres out of 897 in the public system; and 221 out of 264 centres in the private system.
Source: Elaboration by Dioikema Ricerche on Dioikema Information System figures, 1990.

of the formal system. And in some provinces there are worries that the educational potential built up by the formal sector over many years of experience may be eroded.

The survey of the continuing professional education of engineers mentioned in the Canadian contribution indicates that the commercial sector is basically concerned with management rather than with more technical matters. Its growth raises the question of the quality of its services. In Switzerland, public authorities have recourse to these providers because of insufficient teaching staff in higher education institutions. As these examples show, training enterprises have already assumed a major role by filling the gaps left open by other providers. Their role will continue to grow. Should other providers relinquish certain areas of education and training to the commercial sector, or should there be a co-ordinated effort?

Unions

The formal role of unions in the continuing professional education of highly-qualified personnel has always been relatively negligible, and mainly focused on further training opportunities for less skilled adults, and on paid leave for training purposes. The contractual and/or consensual policies of some Member countries, however, do not lead trade unions to play a general role in continuing education. In France, for example, continuing education is governed both by the law and by collective bargaining, which plays a key role since all continuing education is based on inter-industry agreements entered into by the trade unions and employers' associations. These agreements are subsequently adopted by the legislative authorities, and apply to all employees. Unions and employers' associations thus play a key role in formulating statutory rules and regulations as well as in managing the funds for continuing education, thereby sharing power with management and government.

In the Netherlands, a consensus on shared responsibilities has been achieved, based on the principle that "the beneficiary pays". After agreeing on this consensus, the government has set up the Central Manpower Service Board (CBA) to assist in its implementation. Unions are therefore more heavily involved in intervention and positive participation. The government is responsible for the education and training which benefit the community as a whole, while enterprises are responsible for the education and training of benefit to a company or its employees.

In the Nordic countries, the unions have a long tradition of participating in efforts for social and economic modernisation. Collaborative practices have caused unions to involve themselves in continuing education of company personnel as well as of union managers. In some cases, the differences between professional associations and unions are not always easy to grasp. In Finland, for example, holders of academic degrees have a powerful central confederation which includes homogeneous and influential "unions" of doctors, lawyers and teachers. In relation to government, these unions behave exactly like workers' trade unions. In other countries, structures do not overlap; a professional association deals with, for example, lawyers' interests, regardless of economic branches, while unions deal with issues related to a single specific profession, where lawyers could be represented as "white-collar workers", managers or executive personnel.

Non-profit associations

In most Member countries, non-profit associations have historically been involved primarily in popular or "second chance" continuing education. However, they are being drawn into the market for vocational training because of general market conditions and, more particularly, vocational training market conditions. This may lead them to review their position in the continuing education market, including facilities for the highly-qualified, as has happened in France, for instance, with the Association pour l'emploi des cadres (Executive Employment Association). Generally, they are only rarely concerned with highly-qualified personnel, however. The continuing education of the greatest number and the least skilled should not neglect the significance of the continuing education of supervisory staff, if only because they are crucial actors in continuing education policies aimed at the least skilled.

Only one country, the former Yugoslavia explicitly mentions chambers of commerce as providing education and training for managers, but it is highly likely that activities of this kind are widespread.

Higher education

Member countries have different institutional approaches to higher education: the United Kingdom has its universities, polytechnics and colleges; France its

Grandes Ecoles and *Instituts Universitaires de Technologie,* and Germany its universities and *Fachhochschulen*. As these institutions consider continuing professional education, its relationship to their major missions raises important questions.

The introduction to this report pointed out the need to distinguish between initial higher education which has been reorganised to cater for the demands of non-traditional clienteles, and continuing professional education specially created and organised for highly-qualified personnel. Open universities which enable young persons and experienced adults to pursue programmes organised along different lines with course content drawn from initial higher education are one example of successful reorganisation. However, neither this nor the post-graduate Masters-type education aimed at degree-holders with years of professional experience can be defined as continuing professional education. And even if reorganised initial higher education and continuing professional education could conceivably figure among the missions of adult higher education, their issues, funding, access and certification would diverge. In fact, institutions of higher education might even directly compete with other providers of short-term courses in a variety of subjects for the continuing professional education of employed, highly-qualified personnel.

Internal policies of institutions of higher education recognise only tenuous links between academic disciplines and continuing professional education. Although the explanations differ from country to country, these institutions have not been heavily involved in continuing professional education. Institutions of higher education have long-term commitments to skill formation and to the spread of knowledge, and a monopoly on the certification process which enjoys universal social and professional recognition. Their research and educational expertise is much more extensive than that of other providers, and has not yet been put into the service of newly emerging needs.

The situation is difficult to assess quantitatively, not only because criteria differ and are not comparable (numbers of participants, funding methods, legal status of training agencies, etc.) but also because countries describe rather than quantify information on market shares, more often giving an order of magnitude than a precise figure.

Germany, for example, mentions that, in terms of the "number of courses offered", institutions of higher education account for between 5 and 10 per cent of the market for continuing professional education. Austria states that schools and universities "play a minor role". France mentions that despite all it has in its favour, higher education still has only a small share of the continuing professional education market, *i.e.* about 2 per cent of total national funding and 5 per cent of the trainees (see Annex 1, Table A.3). In most cases, and excluding higher education, corporate sector providers predominate on the market for continuing professional education, accounting for over 50 per cent in terms of funding (see Annex 1, Table A.4). In the case of France, the availability of regular statistics on continuing education means that the training market can be analysed on the basis of three criteria. However, a range of criteria are needed to reflect the complexity of the situation[2] (see Annex 1, Table A.5). Sweden mentions the limited involvement of universities and colleges in professional training (see Annex 1, Table A.6).

By contrast, in the United Kingdom a survey among employers carried out by the Training Agency highlighted the predominance of higher education institutions in continuing advanced-level training courses. This is probably due to the expansion of the PICKUP Programme (see below). However, these data do not differentiate between adult education and continuing professional education for highly-qualified personnel (see Annex 1, Tables A.7 and A.8). In the United States, the higher education sector (public and private) accounts for about 26 per cent of the market for continuing education (which does not mean that the same figure applies to continuing professional education) (see Annex 1, Table A.9). Lastly, in the case of Canada, market share is estimated at around 30 per cent and the Canadian report differs from that of other countries in that it considers that higher education institutions have established a strong position for themselves on the market for continuing professional education.

Data clarification is necessary for future continuing education and continuing professional education policies as well as for defining the role of institutions of higher education in this area.

Canada is an exception because higher education provides a major portion of training, and warrants attention. Continuing education of highly-qualified personnel is basically a function of the formal sector, including community colleges, institutes of technology and universities, while professional associations trail with 15 per cent (Table 8).

This situation is due to a combination of several factors:

a) a decentralised approach to education and continuing education. Responsibilities rest basically with the provincial and territorial governments, while federal authorities are more heavily concerned in questions relating to continuing education and employment;

b) participation in continuing education is an individual decision and Canada has opted for an incentive policy targeting individuals rather than fiscal and financial measures aimed at companies;

c) traditionally, companies do not much concern themselves with continuing education.

Table 8. **Canada: involvement of providers in continuing professional education (80 replies)**

Universities	28
Professional organisations	15
Corporations/industry	14
Regional/Community Colleges	13
School districts	10

Source: Cross-Canada Survey of Continuing Professional Education, CAUCE, 1991.

Training enterprises (the commercial sector) are the least engaged in education and training programme planning and implementation. This sector concerns itself with training which costs little and its adaptability and flexibility may impair its innovative capacity. Professional associations and corporations occupy an intermediate position between higher education institutions and the commercial sector.

Canada points out that the budgetary restrictions of the late 1970s did not always benefit continuing education in higher education institutions. For instance, institutions responsible for the initial education of engineers failed to accept any major responsibility for their continuing professional education. In most cases, they made initial education accessible to part-time students but, for continuing education, they left programme design to individual professors. In addition, the educational demand of highly-qualified personnel in higher education institutions is growing and is focusing on custom-made provision convenient to full-time personnel. The Canadian contribution mentions several examples of distance education targeting adults, which is crucially important in a country where educational leave is not traditionally granted, and where there are no tax incentives for corporations. This contribution notes that the higher education institutions will have to include continuing education among their missions, along with initial education and research. It will also be necessary to examine the status of teaching staff, and to provide incentives to improve its commitment to further training activities.

Relatively weak general commitment

In the majority of the other Member countries, the commitment of higher education, until recently rather lukewarm, has increased in the past few years. Occupational aspects of education are gaining priority, and public authorities in many countries are demanding that institutions of higher education make a special effort in confronting fundamental questions.

Italy provides an interesting example of thriving growth – particularly in the private sector – of "Masters"- type programmes, *i.e.* education for updating university graduates with one or two years of professional experience. In the absence of any form of recognition and any officially sanctioned issue (Tables 9 and 10), the growth of this education poses the issue of its quality and equivalence to university education. ASFOR (Associa-

Table 9. **Italy: higher continuing professional education, in the private system: breakdown of education activities by final certification**[a]

	None	Certificate of attendance	Certificate of qualification	Certificate of specialisation	Ex lege
Number	5	1 513	59	56	1
Percentage	0.3	92.6	3.6	3.4	0.1

a) Figures refer to 1 634 out of 8 954 courses.
Source: Elaboration by Dioikema Ricerche on Dioikema Information System figures, 1990.

Table 10. **Italy: higher continuing professional education in the public system: breakdown of education activities by final certification**

	At work		At work/in service		In service		Total	
	n.	%	n.	%	n.	%	n.	%
None	10	18.2	38	69.1	7	12.7	55	100
Certificate of attendance	418	42.1	22	2.2	553	55.7	993	100
Certificate of qualification	1 355	87.2	43	2.8	156	10.0	1 554	100
Certificate of specialisation	337	51.1	66	10.0	257	38.9	660	100
Ex lege	10	26.3	10	26.3	18	47.4	38	100
Total	2 130	64.5	179	5.5	991	30.0	3 300	100

Source: Elaboration by Dioikema Ricerche on Dioikema Information System figures, 1990.

zione per la Formazione alla Direzione Aziendale – Association for Training in Corporate Management), which lists organisations offering MBA courses on the basis of criteria such as the length of education and training, the structure of the teaching staff, and their ability to find posts for at least 80 per cent of their graduates within six months after graduation, is examining the problem. This education responds to precise demands from professionally committed young adults but does not present the same challenges as continuing professional education.

In the United Kingdom, the central government acts through various government agencies to guide all activities of higher education institutions. As far as continuing professional education is concerned, centralisation imposes powerful constraints from which the universities are endeavouring to free themselves by diversifying their sources of finance, and by applying a cost-price policy to a large portion of long-term education. The proportion of long-term university continuing education, including the Open University, is greater than that supplied by other providers, including, in particular, non-university institutions, accounting for about 60 per cent of this type of post-graduate education in 1986/87 (Table 11). The growth of this education and that of short-term education do not equal the level in Polytechnics and Colleges during the 1980s, but universities are proposing major innovations. These include more flexible education, modular systems, credit systems, the possibility of credit transfers, and especially linkages with the training offered by employers, etc. These changes satisfy professions and employers, who are very much in favour of modular systems and credit transfers. The prevailing university certification system, for instance, has been substantially modified to give it greater flexibility, and bring it into line with the structures proposed by the Council for National Academic Awards (CNAA) (*cf.* Chapter III).

The trend in fund allocation underlines the movement towards occupational (work-based) education, in particular under the pressure of programmes like PICKUP. When evaluating the PICKUP programme, the universities established that enrolments in continuing professional education had increased by 20-25 per cent between 1987 and 1988.

Table 11. **United Kingdom: number of first-year mature home post-graduate students, 1986-87**[a]

	Men	Women	Total
Full-time[b]			
University	5 800	3 900	9 700
Polys and college	2 400	2 000	4 400
Higher education	8 200	5 900	14 100
Part-time[b]			
University	6 900	3 800	10 700
Polys and college	5 400	2 700	8 100
Higher education	12 300	6 500	18 800
Full-time and part-time[b]			
University	12 700	7 700	20 400
Polys and colleges	7 900	4 700	12 600
Higher education	20 600	12 400	33 000

a) Mature post-graduates are 25 or over on the first year of their course (ages as of previous August).

b) Undercounted, because the Open University and the University of Buckingham are excluded. In 1988, the Open University admitted 1 142 new full- and part-time post-graduate students, virtually all of whom will be mature (Open University, 1990, Table 10).

Source: Department of Education and Science, 1988, *Statistical Bulletin 11/88*, August, Table 3.

After continuing professional education in medicine, the greatest demand is in business administration and law (37 per cent of participants in 1987/88), education (16 per cent), languages (12 per cent) and engineering (10 per cent). These four subject areas account for 75 per cent of the training courses offered within the framework of the PICKUP programmes.

In the Netherlands, various obstacles explain why public-sector higher education does not occupy a very important position in the training market, including the lack of a close relationship with the professional world, and of organised networks for creating such a rapprochement. Generally speaking, public-sector training needs to improve its image to win a place in the market for continuing professional education, which calls for the elimination of certain financial and statutory restrictions which the teaching staff view as the main obstacle to its involvement in continuing education. Various institutions have already taken measures aimed at decentralising continuing education, and have set up independent commercially-run centres. Access to public-sector institutions is a further difficulty because it is entirely based on academic criteria which also govern teaching and certification. As the Canadian contribution comments, "We should never forget that our clients are not students in the traditional sense; they are working professionals for whom continuing education is part-time and coming to campus has little additional benefit for them".

Non-university higher education

In countries where higher education is divided into university and non-university, there is often a different degree of institutional involvement in continuing professional education. It may seem that non-university institutions have been more active in providing continuing professional education but, as shown in Norway, most continuing professional education courses in universities are for health and education professions, which are not included in the present study. If universities do not offer initial business administration and engineering education, they cannot be expected to provide continuing professional education for engineers, accountants and managers. These fields are often left to specialised institutions, confusingly enough classified differently in different countries. They almost all belong to the "non-university" sector: Polytechnics and Colleges in the United Kingdom and Belgium, short-term regional colleges in Norway (where the long-term courses are classified as "university").

Non-university higher education has been vocational in nature from the start with close ties to the world of work. Continuing education activities fully fit into the conception of these institutions and it is generally recognised that over the past few years short-term non-university institutions have provided a growing percentage of continuing professional education. Unfortunately, no quantitative data exist to indicate the magnitude of the phenomenon. It is certain that these institutions focus their education and training efforts on occupational goals (updating and refresher courses). Since it has come into being more recently, non-university higher education has not yet achieved a level of development like that in universities and, in this sense, it may be claimed that it provides only modest continuing education. The gap is narrowing, however, and competition is growing in areas such as management, business, engineering and information technology.

In the United Kingdom, prior to the merger between universities, Polytechnics and Colleges, the Polytechnics and Colleges were among the leading providers of post-graduate continuing education for those 25 and over at entry (Table 11). In general, the 1980s saw institutional changes which gave new impetus to non-university institutions. Their active involvement in part-time and continuing education, together with their links with industry, have provided a basis for new forms of collaboration (OECD, 1990*d*). They have also played an appreciable role in the continuing professional education of women.

In Japan, there are now signs that institutions of higher education are becoming more heavily committed to occupational-based education. This interest is centred on non-university institutions and, more particularly, on Special Training Schools, which ensure that their continuing education courses are vocational (Dore and Sako, 1989). An examination of the numbers of "students" enrolled in these schools shows that the engineering and business departments consist very largely of employed adults bearing the cost of their own complementary education and training (Table 12).

The Netherlands drew attention to the responsibility for initial education borne by non-university institutions (Higher Vocational Sector), more closely linked to the world of work and to local communities, and to the previously mentioned financial and statutory restraints to explain the emergence of independent education and training centres. Simi-

Table 12. **Japan: extension courses of Special Training Schools (STS): number of students by employment/schooling status**

	Total number of students	Employed			of wich:				
		Total	Paid by employer	Other	Total	Enrolled in other school			Other
						Senior high school	2-year college	4-year college	Other
Engineering	10 698	4 575	1 533	3 042	1 842	1 093	297	373	79	4 281
Agriculture	474	206	–	206	268	262	4	2	–	–
Health-related	2 091	698	231	467	33	12	5	–	16	1 360
Public health	13 728	10 107	3 722	6 385	727	426	180	83	38	2 894
Education/social service	1 680	1 109	33	1 076	280	–	267	13	–	291
Business	27 666	12 860	964	11 896	5 637	340	889	3 452	956	9 169
Home science	13 375	3 982	344	3 638	513	86	155	120	152	8 880
Culture/liberal arts	63 141	9 844	904	8 940	31 232	24 540	457	1 733	4 502	22 065

Source: Ministry of Labour, Report of the Survey on Corporative Education and Training, 1986.

larly, in those Austrian provinces without a university, "adult education centres" aimed at plugging the obvious gaps in the continuing professional education market have been established. They co-operate with universities, and an interesting compensatory policy launched by the public authorities is under way.

Open and distance education

These institutions play a considerable part in continuing adult education and second-chance opportunities. A trend towards occupational courses is noticeable in this area.[3]

However, while many countries mention open and distance education as a way of meeting the demands for continuing professional education (Canada, Denmark, Norway, Sweden, former Yugoslavia), only two contributions give detailed consideration to the subject.

In Germany, reunification is changing the situation. The role of distance education varies from one *Land* to another. There are various providers, but relatively few enrolled students (3 per cent of students enrolled for degree courses). By contrast, in the former eastern Germany, 48 working days a year were legally allowed for continuing education, and distance education was developed in the 1950s to meet the demand of technical courses for personnel, assuming the status of a "second educational track" during the 1970s. Distance education, together with continuing education, were two of the missions undertaken by higher education.

As the harmonization of the eastern and western parts of the country progresses, the importance of distance education will probably continue to be strengthened. The urgent and increasing demand for continuing education in the former German Democratic Republic will continue in future years. Previous structures will be used to provide education which is in line with economic, political and social developments. The report refers to the urgent need to overhaul course content and materials used in economics, management, information technology, the social sciences and law. In the more technical and scientific disciplines, updating is necessary but does not involve the same upheavals, which means that these courses could rapidly be used country-wide. It is likely that individuals will have to pursue education and training activities on their own time. Allocation of funds between the state, the economic partners and individuals will have to be reviewed.

Notwithstanding the changes, some pieces of the former eastern Germany tradition of distance education should be preserved: the educational responsibilities of higher education institutions and staff for direct and distance education and for initial and continuing education; the enormous coverage of the existing distance education; the organisation of short training sessions held during working hours; lastly, the opportunities for transfers between the various sectors of higher education.

The contribution by the Commission of the European Communities, based on a questionnaire submitted to member States and on interviews, defines distance learning as all forms of study which are not under the continuous and immediate supervision of a teacher present in the classroom with his or her students. It is often but not necessarily "open" in the sense that it is more flexible and admission is simplified.

The report notes the rapid growth in distance education over the last ten years or so, and its potential in Eastern Europe in the short term. The contribution focuses attention on small- and medium-sized enterprises (SMEs) which experience difficulties making time and funds available for the education and training strategies, and for which distance education is considered to be a particularly relevant aspect of continuing professional education. Recourse to open and distance education generally diminishes with the size of the enterprise. To understand the modest involvement of SMEs, one has to remember that they recruit few university graduates. Because their supervisory and managerial staff have often "risen from the ranks" because of professional experience and readiness for on-the-job training, they are not particularly interested in training and continuing education in general, or in the potential of open or distance education. On the other hand, several open universities (in Germany, the Netherlands, the United Kingdom, Spain, Portugal and Ireland) indicate that many of their students are employees of small-and medium-sized enterprises who voluntarily and independently undertook continuing education. The lack of recognition of given skills and competences acquired outside traditional educational structures is often mentioned as a disincentive. The idea of a European system of recognition and credit transfers (European Credit Transfer Scheme) was put forth.

The two reports confirm the growth in open and distance education, and draw attention to its potential: access for new clients, and custom-made education and training. These contributions must be seen against the backdrop of a diversified higher education system. In practical terms, both contributions emphasize the urgent need to set up information networks about the supply and demand of education and training facilities, and about the recognition of skills and competences.

Other criteria determining the segmentation

Other factors explain segmented continuing professional education, although no data support their factual existence:

a) funding;
b) educational and training level;
c) discipline;
d) professional sector.

Funding

Generally speaking, the methods of funding continuing education vary widely from country to country and affect how easily and quickly continuing professional education of highly-qualified personnel can develop. For instance, financial burden-sharing between enterprises, public authorities and individuals is very variable and situations contrast sharply. In Germany, the burden is borne essentially by higher education institutions and the individuals; in the United Kingdom, the policy implemented over the last ten years makes the various users bear the costs for long- and short-term occupational education and training; in France, a large share of the funding is provided by enterprises (under the 1971 legislation). The "beneficiary pays" principle is implicitly shared by many Member countries, even though few have genuinely applied it. It is evident that for this category of education, enterprises have a heavy financial commitment. In the United Kingdom, funds provided by individuals, industry and the local authorities are increasing substantially as the share borne by universities and joint funds decreases, reflecting reduced fiscal resources for subsidising traditional adult education. It is interesting to note the distribution of the main sources of finance used for short-term continuing education provided by universities (Table 13). In France, the 1971 legislation obliges firms with ten or more employees to contribute a minimum amount (a percentage of their payroll) to continuing professional education but employers are not compelled to provide training themselves. More recently, under the terms of an Act dated 31 December 1991, compulsory contribution was extended to firms with fewer than 10 employees and the principle of "co-investment" was introduced. Employees contribute to the cost of the training by agreeing to do 25 per cent of it during their free time and without additional salary. In exchange, the unions gained a number of concessions in the form of recognition of the qualifications acquired (promotion and higher pay). Similar arrangements probably already exist in other Member countries and it is likely that the increasing demand from adults for continuing education will lead towards sharing the burden and costs.

It would be interesting to examine the financial consequences for institutions of higher education of the new continuing education policies. In Canada, they clearly benefit

Table 13. **United Kingdom: short-term continuing education provision by universities,**[a] **1983/84 to 1988/89**

Number of courses by principal source of finance

	1983/84	1984/85	1985/86	1986/87	1987/88	1988/89
Private individual fees	2 179	2 539	2 519	2 900	4 152	4 438
UK industry and commerce	1 129	1 369	1 463	1 704	2 069	3 033
Local government	832	885	881	1 139	1 594	1 713
University	829	631	591	721	719	982
Joint university/other funding	10 849	11 062	11 326	11 912	11 065	11 414
Health and social security departments	3 438	3 561	3 774	4 069	3 404	7 071
Other government departments	632	825	779	1 018	882	869
Overseas	263	308	323	306	327	438
Other	366	537	385	449	757	890
Total	20 567	21 713	22 041	24 218	24 969	30 848

a) Excluding the Open University and the University of Buckingham.
Sources: Universities Statistical Record (1985), Vol. 3, Table 17, University Statistics, 1983-84. Universities Statistical Record (1986*b*), Vol. 3, Table 17, University Statistics, 1984-85. Universities Statistical Record (1987*b*), Vol. 3, Table 17, University Statistics, 1985-86. Universities Statistical Record (1988*a*), Vol. 3, Table 19, University Statistics, 1986-87. Universities Statistical Record (1989), Vol. 3, Table 19, University Statistics, 1987-88. Universities Statistical Record, (Proof a), Vol. 3, Table 19, University Statistics, 1988-89.

in terms of their market share of continuing professional education, due to the policy adopted by the public authorities, who have not targeted corporations fiscally (except in Quebec) and have promoted individual commitment.

In addition, the financial resources allocated to provinces and localities have also favoured the more flexible commercial sector. Apart from reactions connected with quality, this measure raises the question of indirect public funding of the private sector (commercial, or profit-making associations or enterprises). The Canadian contribution therefore draws attention to the erosion by the public authorities of the education and training provisions and facilities supplied by the formal sector at the very time that they are funding the other sector. This phenomenon can be found in many countries.

Education and training levels

Levels of education and training also segment continuing professional education for highly-qualified personnel although the lack of information about characteristics of training levels makes it difficult to expand on this. The skill and competence of the targeted personnel determine sources of finance, and pedagogy. In some cases, professional experience is taken into account, and education and training are then probably pragmatically segmented by "levels of education and training" as an academic label. Questions of this kind have been addressed in Sweden, and are currently under consideration, in different terms, in the United Kingdom and Australia. This may touch on the issue of a distinction between initial education adapted to adult requirements and continuing professional education.

Discipline

Disciplines are sufficiently well established so that all or most of the education provided functions homogeneously. Business management, for example, is a sufficiently well-established and structured domain to occupy a segment of the training market, and it does so in the United States. It is difficult to ascertain whether disciplines, or domains of study, or client demands – made through the "institutional" providers in the market – structure the training offer. The case of the Canadian engineers provides a good illustration of the "discipline" effect. Where institutions of higher education dominate the continuing professional education market, they are not very involved in continuing education for engineers partly because of their traditional role in initial training. In countries where universities have no role in the initial education of engineers, they will have very little to do with their continuing education.

The German examples show that it is sometimes difficult to distinguish between the effect of disciplines and that of professional associations. Continuing professional education is segmented into areas such as medicine, law, business, and engineering. But these areas subsume a number of disciplines which are more employment-oriented than the traditional academic disciplines. The Austrian case suggests that giving a discipline a "vocational" slant from the beginning of education can be a catalyst for generating continuing education activities in higher education institutions. This point is stressed and occurs in Norway, for example. However, and perhaps secondary, is the powerful impact of professional associations. The teaching profession is a striking example because it is not bonded by a single discipline, but nonetheless acts as a professional group.

Sectors of professional activity

Organisation by professional areas and/or sectors becomes a segmentation criterion once continuing education responds to a range of needs of comparable enterprises and is sufficiently developed to generate an "explicit education and training policy". In France, the metal or electronics sector could fit this definition. In Germany, the internalisation or externalisation of continuing education is partly linked to industrial policies: internal education exists in the chemical industry, but enterprises have recourse to outside expertise while retaining overall control of the training process. In the construction sector, external training originates mainly from other providers to fill the gaps of enterprises.

The three market sectors

It is difficult to generalise about a "continuing professional education market" for highly-qualified personnel, since its existence and level of development varies according to country. However, setting aside a few countries where the links between higher education and the world of work are still particularly tenuous – Spain, Portugal, the ex-Yugoslavia – the general trend is towards growth, if not "explosion". In the United States, for example, where no national legislation governs education in general, there is national concern about quality and competitiveness, and consequently the public authorities have become increasingly interested in the continuing professional education of the labour force. The situation is consequently characterised by explosive overall growth in provider initiatives (US Department of Labor, 1985; US Department of Education, 1985). Providers who "mould" and "structure" the market in different Member countries fulfil different functions and warrant close examination.

Describing the market and how it operates requires scrutinising the roles and relationships of different providers. We will pin-point certain key issues facing public authorities responsible for higher education as well as the economic and social partners. Providers will be grouped according to the following key features (Table 14):

- definition of an educational strategy;
- scientific and technological potential;
- clientele;
- source of finance;
- nature of training;
- type of certificate.

Criteria for describing the market distinguish three very different training sectors: formal, non-formal, and commercial.

Table 14. **Characteristics of the three sectors of continuing education**

Key features	Formal sector	Non-formal sector	Commercial sector
1. Educational strategy	Education policy is explicit and is part of its primary vocation.	Any possible training policy comes under the heading of human resource management or the protection of professional interests to which it is subordinated.	No educational strategy, strictly commercial.
2. Scientific and technological potential	Scientific, technological research and development potentials exist and are linked to educational possibilities.	Generally, there is no scientific potential as such, but there may be research and development capacities.	No scientific or technological potential, no research and development facilities.
3. Clientèle	Comes from outside.	Internal.	Canvassed outside.
4. Sources of financing	Generally, financed from public or mixed sources (public/private).	Financing is private.	Private financing.
5. Nature of the training	Traditional, with flexible time arrangements adapted for working adults. Training provided is more and more of short duration.	Short and custom-designed training courses.	Short-term training courses.
6. Certification	Certification is based on traditional academic recognition – knowledge-based. There are some efforts towards recognition of non-academic skills.	When it exists, certification takes the form of "certificates of attendance" and sometimes recognises experiential competences.	A "certificate of attendance" is the general rule.

Source: D. Colardyn, OECD.

The formal sector

This encompasses university and non-university institutions of long- and short-term higher education, distance education, etc., institutions traditionally considered to belong to higher education and whose principal mission is initial higher education, research in the case of the universities, and sometimes applied research and development in the vocationally-oriented non-university institutions. Usually, these institutions are basically publicly funded, although their sources of finance can be mixed (public/private). Clients come from outside and take courses whose content still closely mirrors that of initial higher education, although there are more short-term courses. Certification, which is specific to this sector, is based on traditional academic discipline-specific recognition, with some effort to recognise non-academic, or experiential competences and skills.

The non-formal sector

Comprised of enterprises, professional associations, unions and non-profit associations whose primary mission is not (higher or other) education, but the production or the defence of professional interests. For these organisations, training is an aspect of human resource management and/or maintaining and promoting a professional category, and is moulded by these professional considerations. Continuing education here is a strategy subordinated to non-educational policies. Research and development capacities do exist in some cases (large corporations), but they are essentially directed towards production. The participating personnel belong to the corporation, the professional association or the union. Funds are mainly, though not exclusively, private (partnerships). Continuing education bears a clear vocational stamp, and courses are increasingly custom-made and of short duration. Certificates, if there are any, often record attendance, and a current is developing which favours the recognition of experiential competences and skills, especially within the framework of partnerships with higher education institutions.

The commercial sector

This comprises various types of educational enterprises which pursue a commercial strategy without concern for developing an educational policy. Selling education for profit distinguishes this sector from the others. There is no research and development potential. Involvement in the continuing professional education of highly-qualified personnel is basically centred on areas necessitating modest material investments (communications, management), or very substantial material investment (information technology) often provided by the training enterprise's parent company. The clientele is recruited from outside, it does not arrive voluntarily, and it is geographically scattered. Funding is probably exclusively private. Training is short-term, and the certificates are usually records of attendance.

Table 14 shows that these three sectors are developed to varying degrees, and that the dynamic generated between them characterises the market for continuing professional education. In some countries, the formal and non-formal sectors prevail or dominate, in which case, they "provide", "structure", "mould" and "govern" the supply of education and training. Such countries frequently refer to the private sector or system as something opposed to the public sector or system (Italy, the Netherlands). In other cases, the commercial sector already has a sufficiently long and established history for it to function as a full-fledged element of the continuing professional education market, on which it has a palpable influence (the United Kingdom, the United States, France, Norway). The contributions of the German-speaking countries and Switzerland do not enable to evaluate its extent, or its real or potential consequences on the dynamic between the sectors (Germany, Austria). Generally, and given the enormous difficulties quantifying the phenomenon, it is evident that the growth and vocational slant of education and training are basically determined by the activities of the non-formal and commercial sectors. Usually, and with few exceptions (Canada, the United States), the positions and roles of institutions of higher education remain weak, and their missions still ill-defined.

How the training market functions

In most of the countries under consideration, continuing professional education of highly-qualified personnel is dominated by the non-formal (enterprises and associations) and commercial sectors.

The continuing professional education market is very different from that of the initial education systems where public authorities bear the primary responsibility, and from the market for the continuing education of the less skilled where public authorities often have a large share of responsibility which they share for a variety of reasons with the non-formal sector (enterprises, unions and non-profit associations).

Regarding the continuing professional education of highly-qualified personnel, the growing commercial sector is generating a new dynamic between sectors and changing the market: the formal sector is no longer confronted merely by a thriving non-formal sector seeking collaboration, but by a diametrically opposed commercial sector which is altering the traditional balance.

Italy and the Netherlands illustrate this new balance. In Italy, the education and training supply structure reveals a clearly-defined market "rupture" between a formal (public) sector and the other two privately funded training sectors. The formal, or public, sector is chiefly concerned with the unemployed, and, to a lesser extent, provides long-term continuing education. It devotes little effort to higher education (in terms of numbers of courses, numbers of hours of instruction and numbers of participants). By contrast, the private sectors specialise in short-term courses for the employed. University-level education and training receives greater attention. The continuing education world is polarised between the formal sector, including the regulated public system, and the more flexible and rapidly expanding sectors with private funding. Their coexistence is not conducive to a healthy market for continuing education or continuing professional education in which quality and effectiveness of the education and training supply are adversely affected.

In the Netherlands, the public and private, or commercial, sectors now compete, and the limits between their activities are sometimes blurred. The commercial sector has benefited from the inability of the public sector to respond quickly, effectively, and appropriately to the needs of enterprises confronted by structural change. Because these enterprises doubt the ability of the public sector to respond quickly and appropriately, they view the commercial sector positively. The commercial sector is therefore playing an increasingly important role in occupationally-oriented education and training.

The central issue of continuing professional education is not merely educational, but also involves the responsibilities of the social and professional partners in the skill formation of the labour force in general, and, in the present case, of highly-qualified personnel.

Various social partners and public authorities play a part in the relationships between the three sectors: "classical" social partners with a role in the social, economic and educational fields, *i.e.* employers and unions (relatively uninvolved with highly-qualified personnel); increasingly important professional associations; public national and regional authorities, the various ministries concerned with questions of continuing education, and the authorities responsible for higher education, where the influence of academic staff is particularly great.

Paradoxically, the commercial sector which has an increasingly prominent role (according to country) is conspicuously absent from the debates. In any event, no such representation is noted in any of the country contributions because, for the time being, this sector does not seek participation in formulating the national education policies of the Member countries.

As the examples demonstrate, the growth of the commercial and longer-standing non-formal sectors reflects the traditional lack of involvement and structural inability of the formal sector to respond to the new demands and needs for continuing professional education. And because of this, the private sectors have enabled the institutions of higher education to concentrate to a greater degree on their specificities.

However, the present situation makes it clear that the pertinent questions can no longer be asked in purely educational terms and debated only among education authorities, as is currently the case in compulsory schooling. Other sectors which, by definition, have non-educational primary objectives and which assess quality differently, are already in the picture.

Do public authorities and the authorities responsible for higher education wish higher education to play a specific role in the continuing professional education of highly-qualified personnel? Discussing the limits of this commitment and putting to practical use the specificities of higher education, are on the agenda. Various forms of learning are recognised, various educational options coexist and each contributes in its own way to the continuing education of the labour force and to the enhancement of national competitiveness. Higher education policies – on higher education and training levels, on continuing professional education of highly-qualified personnel – must be redefined.

The public authorities and the training market functioning

Very schematically put, the dialogue and co-ordination of continuing professional education of highly-qualified personnel in each country differ according to whether governance is centralised, decentralised or centred on the training market; the balance between demand and supply is differently determined. Demand and supply vary according to different principles, communication and division of responsibilities vary between the authorities and the partners (enterprises, unions, professional associations, commercial sector) who participate to varying degrees in policy formulation and implementation. To facilitate the presentation, three "models" follow of countries with different legislative systems reflected culturally and socially in the relationships between the State and the regions, between the public education authorities and between the partners. It is clearly impossible to accommodate all national particularities by these few schematic management characteristics. Moreover, within the same "governance" type, there will be widely varying co-ordination processes which will contribute to the emergence of new, and as yet untried, forms of interaction.

A traditionally centralised context

State (central, public) authorities play the dominant role in legislative and regulatory matters, but may not be the main source of finance (for the professional categories considered in this report). Centralisation permits overall monitoring of the relations between education and employment, may favour certain linkages, although the position of negotiating procedures and the collective role in defining the educational aims are not always clear.

The countries taking part in this project and conforming to this model are Denmark, France, Finland, Italy, Japan and Sweden. The examples are provided by Italy, Finland, Denmark and Sweden where matters relating to continuing professional education are the responsibility of central government departments which draft relevant legislation and monitor its application. Traditionally, such national legislation has partly or completely regulated questions relating to continuing professional education. Recently, application has broadened and there has been more possibility for education and training outside the formal system. In fact, centralised "governance" of continuing professional education is often faced with the continuing professional education market since either the latter has developed outside the centralised, and frequently rigid, formal structures, or the public authorities have urged its development, and may try to integrate it into the formal structures.

In Italy and Finland, a policy of partial decentralisation and privatisation is in place to bring the higher education institutions closer to the world of work. Public authorities are externalising continuing education, while to some degree preserving flexible institutional links. In both countries there is an incipient movement towards a market-centred "governance" model.

Sweden is opting for an approach in which the commercial sector is integrated into higher education on the self-funding principle. Denmark may well follow the same course. Continuing professional education has little tradition behind it, either in higher education or in the world of work. Authorities believe that graduates employed in the private sector will benefit from in-house training, and from education and training provided by professional associations, already very active in this respect, and chambers of commerce. Higher education establishments will be encouraged to develop their offerings to a greater extent and, thanks to the impact of the Open University and distance education, the groups targeted by continuing professional education will be larger and more diversified.

Public authorities wishing to bring higher education and employment closer together, or to divest themselves of some educational functions for which they feel no responsibility or interest, are instigating a drive towards privatisation in these countries which responds to clients' needs for which the formal sector has insufficient regard. The debates bring out the two options which are therefore open to higher education:

- institutions have public authorisation to enter the continuing professional education market in the hope that they will then compete with other providers (in education and training or research), and create conditions conducive to qualitatively improving available services;
- higher education is opened up, but retains some of the characteristics of a public service. The result is a mixed model favouring partnerships; this model seems to have greater appeal in countries as diverse as Italy, France, Finland and Sweden.

The roles of the various partners are not referred to very explicitly. The options vary in the search to develop an approach acceptable to the different "partners". It is true that traditions of tripartite relationships between the social partners are of longer standing in the Nordic countries. An interesting French initiative suggests that consultative mechanisms between the social partners should be set up in higher education. They would be of the same type as those which operate traditionally in relation to initial vocational education at the secondary level (Colloquium at the Sorbonne, 1991). Nevertheless, the structures for dialogue with higher education sometimes fail to take sufficient account of professional associations as fully qualified partners at this level (for highly-qualified personnel).

A traditionally decentralised context

Regional and/or local authorities implement legislation. Higher education therefore usually enjoys a very wide margin of man2vre provided that it complies with the general principles established by the federal authorities. Decentralisation facilitates collaboration between partners, and the possibility of responding to economic (*e.g.* regional) realities.

Countries taking part in the project which conform to this model are Canada, Germany and Austria. Canada is one of the Member countries in which higher education institutions play a major role in continuing professional education.

A crucial key to understanding the situation of continuing professional education in Canada is the low corporate commitment to education and training. To date, responsibility and funding in continuing education and continuing professional education of the labour force have been largely public, and structures have developed within the formal framework which vary with industrial sector and qualification levels. As mentioned before, these factors, together with decentralised organisation, the limited role of federal authorities, and funds channelled towards individual beneficiaries, account for the existence of a formal sector of continuing education and continuing professional education far more substantial than in most other Member countries.

Recently, the federal government, and to a lesser extent the provinces, have used financial means to promote the development of the commercial sector, made up of profit-making training enterprises. This upheaval in educational strategies is not universally accepted, and the rapid growth of this sector is causing the public authorities to regard it with greater caution.

Some time ago, the provincial education authorities voiced the need for improved co-ordination. In 1988, the Council of Ministers proposed that the formulation and implementation of education policies should be considered by a consultative committee made up of provincial and territorial representatives, of the federal government, educational institutions, "voluntary" corporate organisations, the labour force, the students and trainees. This proposal, together with the joint proposal of the Ministry of Employment and Immigration and the Canadian Labour Market and Productivity Centre, led in early 1991 to the creation of the Canadian Labour Force Development Board. This body evaluates training programmes, lays down national standards and budgets, and examines costs of various educational strategies.

In this federal system, two national institutions play a key role in the debates on human resources: the Canadian Labour Market and Productivity Centre and the Economic Council of Canada. The first was established to improve relations and facilitate consultation between employers and employees with a view to stepping up productivity on the basis of continuing professional education policies and strategies. The Economic Council's mission is to consider questions relating to human resource skill formation.

The situation in Germany is totally different. The 1976 legislation (*Hochschulrahmengesetz*), which establishes the missions of higher education, states that institutions of higher education have a statutory obligation to provide continuing education in addition to their research activities and their mission of providing initial higher education from first degree to doctorate. This legislation decrees that the institutions of higher education have to provide continuing academic education programmes; that they have to contribute to the other further training activities offered by other organisations; and that they should also encourage the continuing education of their own staff. The 1966 Austrian legislation (*Allgemeines Hochschulstudiengesetz*) creates a similar situation, and also requires that the missions of universities include the continuing education of graduates – an objective reinforced by the Acts of 1975. By contrast, neither vocational nor general continuing professional education has made hardly any inroads into German or Austrian universities[4] to date. Commitment of higher education is characterised by individual rather than institutional participation, as the Austrian contribution points out. The fact of the matter is that continuing education has so far failed to gain a sufficient foothold in higher education to ensure buoyant development. Differences are disciplinary; professors have always been engaged in continuing professional education as well-paid secondary employment for, although, continuing education (and, within limits, continuing professional education) is included among the missions of higher education, professors see no material advantages in developing it in-house. This system calls for acknowledging the present limits to university commitment to the continuing professional education market.

Regional authorities are responsible for managing continuing professional education; there is an implicit call for a rapprochement between the partners. Countries with a centralised tradition also rely on such a philosophy when they attempt to move towards decentralisation. However, the geographical proximity of the partners in the continuing professional education market does not mean that either their rapprochement or their institutional collaboration will in fact occur.

Various outside pressures favour a greater role for continuing education in the university, seen also as a means of strengthening collaboration with industry: the Education Council (*Deutscher Bildungsrat*), the Scientific Council (*Wissenschaftsrat*), the Vice-chancellors' Conference and the Employers' Association. University professors, however, still have difficulty in regarding continuing professional education as a real mission of higher education whose tradition conflicts with the idea of selling services, even education and training, or competing with other providers in the training market. The argument most often advanced against continuing professional education in higher education is that it would overload degree courses, which really no longer allow any room for education and training of any other kind. Forms of collaboration have recently been taking shape, especially between the university and non-university sectors.

A market context

This applies to countries in which, by economic, social and cultural tradition, the continuing professional education market has neither been regulated nor monitored by the public authorities, and to other countries in which public authorities are issuing regulations that in the shorter or longer term, will be governed by the market. These countries come under one or the other of the two preceding models.

Of the countries taking part in this project, the United Kingdom, the Netherlands and the United States conform to this model. The reasons for the development of the continuing professional education market may vary widely:

a) public authorities wish to broaden the basis of privatisation, without necessarily having collective acceptance from economic and social partners (the United Kingdom);

b) public authorities, together with the various partners, try to awaken public and political awareness with a view to securing a collectively funded commitment (the Netherlands);

c) A *de facto* situation without a clearly defined policy (the United States).

Two considerations have guided the United Kingdom and the Netherlands in this direction: continuing professional education should adhere to the principle that "the beneficiary pays", contrary to compulsory education, where the responsibility of the public authorities is clearly stated; the distinction drawn between continuing education (recurrent education, second chance) and continuing professional education targeting employed highly-skilled adults. As far as the continuing education of the labour force is concerned, public authorities acknowledge their missions and responsibilities. But when it comes to continuing professional education, these are partially transferred to the direct beneficiaries – enterprises, professional associations, unions, the commercial sector and, sometimes, the individuals – who accept them pretty much as a matter of course.

In the United Kingdom, the expansion of continuing professional education since the early 1980s is considered successful, despite persistent shortcomings. The goal of central government has been to involve the professions and industry, and to induce them to make more and greater devising and setting-up of continuing professional education. Parallel to this, the public authorities exerted pressure on the higher education institutions and participated in the start-up funding of numerous education and training services. The creation of the PICKUP programme gave a real impetus to both higher education institutions and companies to commit themselves to continuing professional education with three objectives in view: improving the quantitative and qualitative response to employers' needs; encouraging new methods and approaches; making employers aware of the importance of continuing education.

Thanks to the actions of various public organs such as the Department of Education and Science, the Training Agency and the Department of Trade and Industry, many forms of collaboration have been encouraged to increase the volume of training, to improve its links with the professional environment, to improve the concept of education and training, its delivery, its transferability and the recognition of acquired experience and knowledge.

This delegation of "governance" to the training market has been the subject of deliberations within the public authorities and professional associations (managers and engineers), but there has been no movement towards collective consultation or the establishment of "institutionalised" mechanisms for regular exchanges of viewpoints with the social partners.

In the Netherlands, the central government bears responsibility for educational content (in essence, the quality) and funding; education and training are regarded as investments, for which a price has to be paid. The result is that higher education has greater freedom with regard to content and the methods proposed, and the influence of outside actors is more evident. Public authorities want to gear education more closely to the economy and the labour market; this approach is based on a national consensus, although it raises the issue of the limits of responsibility of the public authorities.

The government is responsible for ensuring sufficient general education, but it has no role in education and training linked to the needs of enterprises. The debate centres on demarcating the limits of each of the actors' function (the government and the social partners) in continuing professional education policy. At the moment, tripartite responsibility is considered to prevail, but the respective roles are not yet clearly delineated. Employers are certainly increasingly conscious of their contributions to the content and funding of training directly aimed at professional life.

In December 1989, the social partners and the government signed a central agreement on a common policy on continuing education and continuing professional education for the entire labour force. At the instigation of the Ministry of Education and Science, a temporary committee on education and employment was set up to formulate recommendations and proposals conducive to an improved relationship between education and employment. This issue is regarded as fundamental in the Netherlands, given the mismatch between initial education and labour's needs, cited by manufacturers as the primary reason for the growth of continuing education. Given the need for urgent action, it is accepted that content, organisation and funding depend on the public authorities and on the social partners. More than ever, the government is making its actions contingent on the participation and consensus of all the economic and social actors.

In the United States, the traditional approach has been to allow unfettered development of the continuing professional education market. This is determined by four basic characteristics: *i)* educational questions are not within the federal purview; *ii)* professional associations have a specially important role in the legislative sphere; *iii)* corporations are primary providers of training, though it is difficult to quantify this accurately; *iv)* higher education establishments are able to benefit financially from their continuing professional education activities, *i.e.* they profit from the services they sell.

These four points explain the growth of the training market, and the difficulty at federal level of gaining any precise idea about the nature of the expansion. Federal difficulties affect the type of data gathered nationally (*cf.* the introduction to the national report of the United States). Analysing the few available, and rather old, national data, the national report confirms the importance of the non-academic providers (corporations, associations, commercial sector) in the continuing professional education market and the predominance of 4-year higher education institutions among the academic providers. Broadly put, employers are estimated to be the prime providers of continuing professional education.

The contribution also draws attention to the roles of the various actors, and to some aspects relevant to the missions of higher education institutions (financial opportunities, chances for research and consultancy, and the improved visibility and credibility of the institution in the eyes of the public). Nevertheless, the federal authorities are conscious of the need to increase the transparency of the market, and to this end are planning to establish databanks and launch new surveys capable of shedding more light on the changes in progress. This change in position of the public authorities springs from the conviction that continuing professional education is an important element in a national strategy focused on the quality of education and training, and on the ability of American society to be competitive in the world economy. As Eurich (1990) points out, the issues raised by the continuing professional education not only of highly-qualified personnel but of the whole labour force call for responsible action by the public authorities. This work underlines the importance of implementing more vigorous federal policies, of improving policies in the individual states, and of encouraging initiatives in the private sector and partnerships between the actors.

Benefits and limitations

Clearly, many actors and partners play a role in the continuing professional education of highly-qualified personnel. These cases exemplify the mechanisms of collaboration and dialogue, now essential to enable the higher education institutions to determine more clearly the limits of their missions regarding continuing professional education, and their roles in adult education in general.

The relationships, tensions, and balance between these three governance systems sectors need to be examined in their national contexts, so that public authorities and education authorities can guide their continuing education (and continuing professional education) policies, set the limits of their commitments, and determine the aspects which they wish to develop. It is immediately clear that higher education policies cannot be examined in isolation from the general context of the training market, and that account has to be taken of the whole range of facilities for university-level education and training.

Notes

1. Survey by the Association of Professional Engineers of Ontario (APEO) 1976, mentioned in the Canadian contribution, 1991.
2. The source for Tables A.3 and A.4 is the "Comptes économiques de la formation continue" and that of Table A.5 is the "Projet de loi de finances". The first source is more comprehensive, which explains the variation in results.
3. For more detailed information, see Germany's contribution, which puts forward some initial ideas about the formulation of a distance education policy common to the two former republics, and a proposal advanced by the Commission of the European Communities for the use by small- and medium-sized enterprises of open and distance education for the continuing education of their highly-qualified personnel.
4. In their contribution, the German authorities have chosen to deal with questions relating to the occupationally-oriented education and training of highly-qualified personnel in terms of the universities, and not within the overall context of the country's higher education system.

Chapter III

Towards a Continuing Professional Education Policy in Higher Education

Which continuing professional education?

As has already become clear, the idea of a market, defined broadly and varying by country, is a useful means of contextualising developments specific to higher education in an overall picture encompassing the economic and social partners. Our methodological approach has already revealed the lack of any precise definition of the missions of higher education in this area. This chapter will round off these deliberations by considering the internal challenges confronting institutions of higher education.

For governments and the economic and social partners to be able to implement a continuing professional education policy, they must first identify all possible forms of adult education and training undertaken in a working life. However, as Austria and others point out, it is not yet easy for countries to clearly distinguish between continuing professional education targeting highly-qualified personnel, and continuing vocational education aimed at other personnel, nor is there always a clear distinction between continuing education's general or vocational nature and, for the highly-qualified, this distinction becomes blurred.

Higher education institutions play a role in the various forms of continuing training mentioned above – general, specialised, designed for the highly-qualified, and courses for adults at the stage of initial higher education (involving part-time study, distance learning and modules). Quantitatively, first-time initial higher education is most common, while rounding off university studies and facilitating transition into working life (*cf.* the growth of "masters" courses) also occurs, in which case education is aimed at young adults, and clearly fits into the framework of initial education.

The examples given below demonstrate the difficulty of distinguishing different types of continuing education from initial higher education. Sometimes, a concern for social justice leads to the setting-up of highly-integrated initial and continuing education systems, as in Sweden for example. Sometimes, on the contrary, the distinction from initial higher education is clearly defined, as in Japan. In other cases, the integration of continuing professional education into the context of higher education involves establishing specialised centres within universities as in Finland, or the implementation of a policy

Graph 1. **SWEDEN: Occupational groups
taking part in personnel education, spring 1989**

(financed by employers and arranged by universities and colleges)

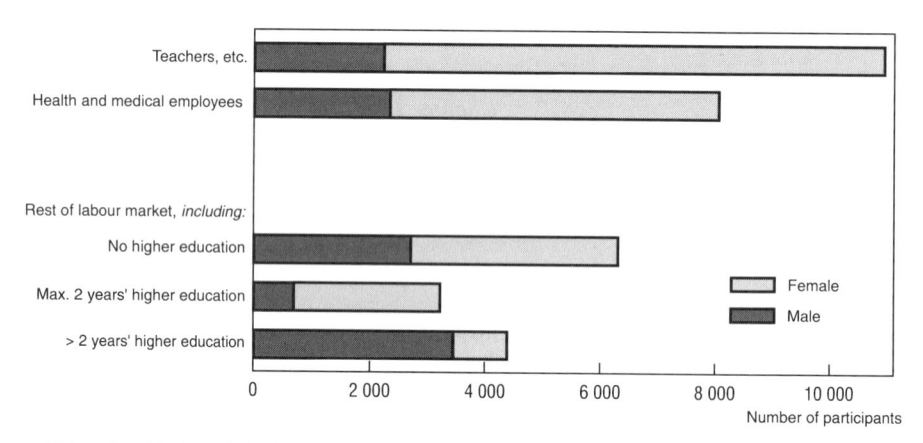

Source: National contribution of Sweden.

based on a national consensus, as in the Netherlands, both countries where there is an explicit political desire to develop relations between higher education and employment with a view to greater coherence.

Sweden's "integrated system" encompasses various forms of further training and continuing education: *i)* that which depends in whole or in part on higher education, *ii)* that which is organised outside the higher education institutions, *i.e.* "personnel education" organised by the employers or other actors (Graph 1). This example sheds light on the complexity of continuing professional education in its relationship to higher (initial) education. There are two cases: either continuing education depends on higher education, or it takes place outside.

In the first case, continuing education depends wholly or partially on higher education. This includes single-subject courses, commissioned education, personnel education and advanced programmes.

Single-subject courses

Single-subject courses are used for both initial and continuing education, depending on what is defined by the legislation. About one-third are attended by students in initial education, while two-thirds fall into the continuing education category. In initial education, young persons attend courses in subject areas for which there is no complete programme, or where they wish to supplement their initial education with non-compulsory courses. The same single-subject courses are available within the framework of continuing education. Funding is public (State) and is managed by the higher education institutions.

In the 1980s, important developments took place in the way students were using single-subject courses. First, a change in age structure was discernible, indicating a new use for these educational opportunities. Some universities found that, gradually, these courses were being taken by younger students instead of complete study programmes. Secondly, there was a tendency to group single-subject courses into a coherent whole mirroring initial higher education. Students who had been unable to enter the form of higher education which they had originally wanted were taking these single-subject courses by way of continuing education, and avoiding the difficulties of selection. What is more, by taking these courses as continuing education, these students were able to combine their studies with part-time employment.

In future years, the consequences of the demographic decline will be largely offset by changes in the qualification structure, and by the growing demand for highly-qualified personnel. The Swedish authorities consider that this will lead to an increased demand for single-subject courses, which may slow down towards the end of the 1990s for young people, while continuing to increase for adults aged 30 to 65.

Commissioned education

A recent feature of the Swedish scene is accommodated within the operation of higher education institutions. Government and parliamentary texts define this as ''the sale of education against special payment in response to a specific demand for education made by a client on behalf of a group of students paid for by that client''. Commissioned education therefore takes place in institutions of higher education on behalf of those who are gainfully employed, and who are seeking education and training through their organisations (firms, government agencies). Such training does not target individuals or young students in initial education; its purpose is to create an area of continuing education which is separate from the initial higher education offered in institutions of higher education.

It can be offered by an institution if its nature and level are in line with the normal activities of that institution; it need not conform to the general programmes; ''advanced'', basic and local programmes can be included under commissioned education, as well as any training facilities specially devised to that end; full cost has to be paid; the objectives must not run counter to those of higher education institutions; such activities must be planned and conducted within the framework of the institution's normal activities; certificates may be awarded if participants meet the conditions applicable to higher education in general.

Personnel education under the auspices of higher education

Little is organised by higher education, companies are responsible for the major share. But it is interesting to note that continuing personnel education targeting those who

Graph 2. **SWEDEN: Overlap between personnel, commissioned and other continuing education, 1988/89**
Round figures, 1 000 whole-year equivalents

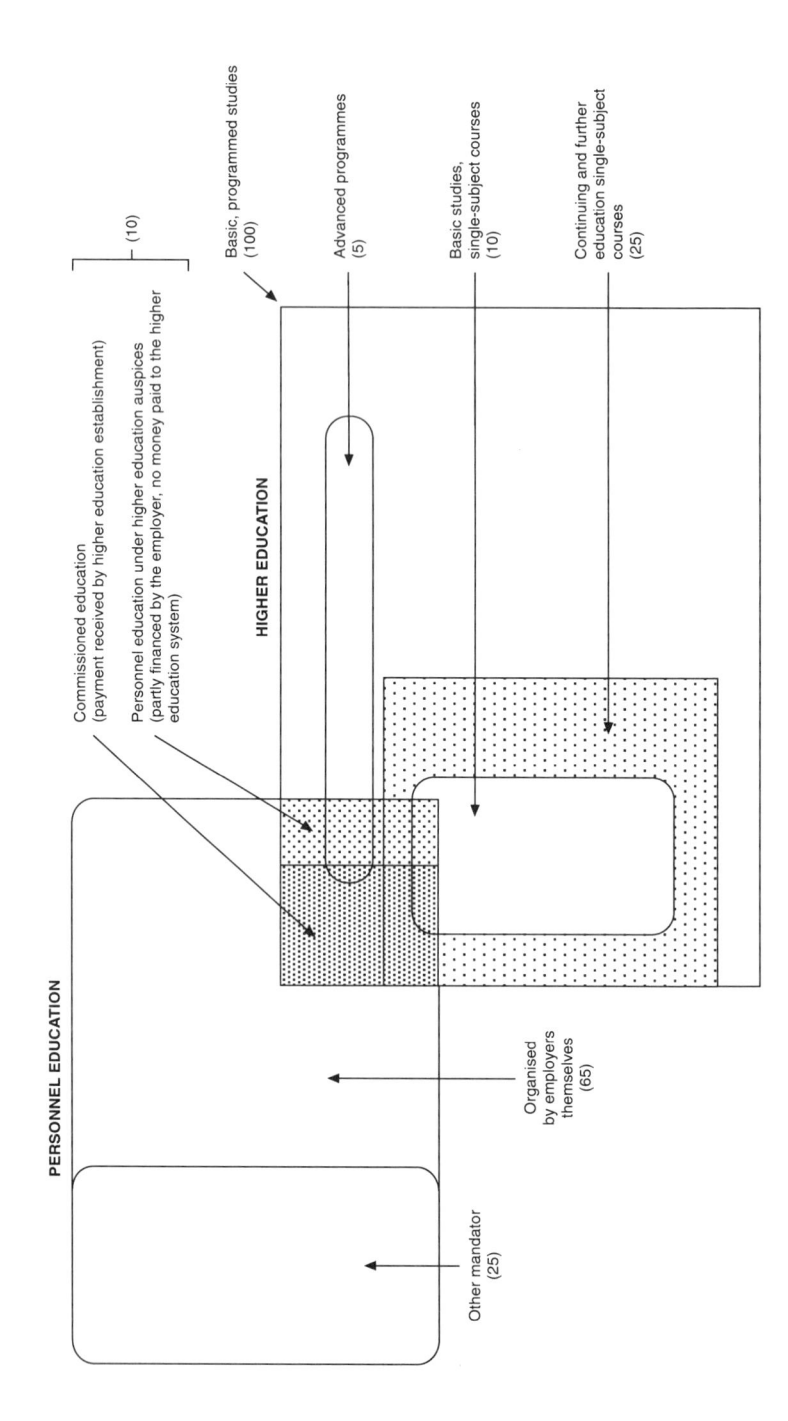

Basic, programmed studies (100)

Advanced programmes (5)

Basic studies, single-subject courses (10)

Continuing and further education single-subject courses (25)

(10)

Commissioned education (payment received by higher education establishment)

Personnel education under higher education auspices (partly financed by the employer, no money paid to the higher education system)

HIGHER EDUCATION

PERSONNEL EDUCATION

Organised by employers themselves (65)

Other mandator (25)

Source: National contribution of Sweden.

have already completed initial higher education is basically designed for males (engineers, senior technicians, scientific workers, economists) (Graph 2).

"Advanced programmes"

These are forms of post-graduate education (ISCED level 7) complying strictly with academic rules.

In this case, personnel education takes place outside higher education. It is organised for over 60 per cent by employers or other providers. Higher education is responsible for only 10 per cent of this employer-funded market (disregarding teachers and the medical and paramedical professions, in which the figures are a little more favourable to higher education) (Table 15). Other providers are basically study circles and associations, both of which have been declining in recent years.

In view of the extensive overlap between initial and continuing education in higher education, and the emergence of "commissioned education", an element with a different character, the Swedish situation illustrates the problems now besetting a strict definition of continuing professional education. We therefore have to turn to those Member countries which have another tradition of continuing education (United States, United Kingdom, Netherlands, France, Finland). Their contributions make it clear that continuing professional education cannot be examined in the same terms as formal initial education.

Japan presents an interesting illustration of this question. Stated very broadly, Japanese employment and education are characterised by three features: lifelong employment, the absence of an adult labour market, the importance of in-house training. The Japanese contribution puts the general situation of lifelong employment into relative terms, and makes it clear that "white-collar" mobility does not differ significantly from that in the United States or Europe. However, as the authors of *Japan at Work* (OECD, 1989d) point out, it is difficult to gain a clear picture of the phenomenon.

For example, integrating continuing professional education into corporate structures is very marked, whether it relates to the training of young graduates entering the corporation, mid-career training, on-the-job training, internal redeployment, or education and training linked to promotion.

Induction training is centred on the corporation, its culture and its operation, specific items of knowledge, and motivation. Young graduates entering the corporation spend one or two weeks becoming familiar with the corporation, one to six months of training and/ or special courses before taking up the position for which they have been recruited (Table 16).

Conditions in Japan are particularly favourable to mid-career or on-the-job training, as "lifelong employment" engenders an active kind of non-formal learning. The use of job rotation or redeployment depends on the size of the enterprise. This type of training targets university rather than high-school graduates (Table 17). Lastly, at the top hierarchical levels, some forms of education and training – management, communication – precede promotion.

Table 15. **Sweden: occupational and educational backgrounds of gainfully employed persons taking part in personnel education financed by employers, 1989**

Converted into whole year equivalents (WTEs) per educational mandator

Mandator	Teachers	Health and medical care employees	Other occupational sectors, including			Total
			No higher education	Max. 2 years' higher education	> 2 years' higher education	
Own employer	42	54	69	66	65	63
College/university	22	21	3	19	9	10
Trade union	1	2	4	–	–	2
Komvux	–	4	4	–	–	3
Other mandators[a]	34[b]	19	20	15	26	22
WTEs 1989 (one year)	8 200	14 000	53 700	12 900	10 100	98 900
Number of participants Spring 1989 (6 months)	170 000	169 000	811 000	134 000	141 000	1 425 000

Dashes in the columns above denote < 0.5%.
a) Including 4 100 WTEs (123 000 participants) with unknown mandators.
b) Including teachers' in-service days (four days per annum, approximately) equalling about 1 500 WTEs (73 000 participants).
Source: Sweden contribution, 1991.

Table 16. **Japan: an example of induction training – Sony Electronics**

April 2	ADMISSION CEREMONY
April 2-9	INTRODUCTION SEMINAR
	Classroom lectures
April 10-September 6	INDUCTION TRAINING I
	(For both administrative and technical recruits)
April 10-27	Basic training
April 10-13	Lectures on basic electronics, analog and digital circuits
April 16-17	Planning and exercise project
April 18-26	Exercise project
April 27	Review
May 1-July 27	Plant and sales practicum
May 1-31	Plant practice
June 1-28	Sales practice
June 29-July 6	Customer service practice
July 9	Administrative recruits are given assignments
July 9-September 7	INDUCTION TRAINING II
	(Technical recruits only)
	Classroom lectures on basic technologies, computer science, outline of major products
September 7	Technical recruits are given assignment

Source: Kyoiku-Kunren Jitsureishu (Examples of training and education) 1989, p. 239.

Self-development and specialised training are matters of more individual responsibility, and are of less concern to the corporation. For the most part, such training comprises short courses on subjects like the introduction of new techniques or regulations. Correspondence course popularity is enhanced by the absence of required previous formal qualification. Finally, private institutions offer personnel education services.

The Swedish and Japanese examples make clear the divergent approaches to continuing professional education of highly-qualified personnel from one Member country to another. This being said, emphasis placed on occupational competences, as compared with academic skills, is growing with a view to maintaining and extending the knowledge, skills and competences linked to professional life. Continuing professional education is becoming an element of human resource management, and a factor in the professional, social and cultural development of the individual. In this scenario, growth in continuing professional education within the formal education system is indissolubly linked to its growth in the "non-formal" and commercial sectors.

Experience in some countries illustrates the transition from a tentative to a strategic vision. As the United Kingdom report has noted, continuing professional education has clear implications for the future, and occupationally-based education and training policies are gradually taking shape. These policies may be regarded as instituting "professional

Table 17. **Japan: corporate policies regarding job rotation**

In percentage

Firm size (number of employees)	Rotate as a means for ability development	Rotate when necessary	Avoid rotation except for filling vacancies	No response
UNIVERSITY GRADUATES				
Administrative				
5 000 or more	66.8	32.8	0.4	–
1 000-4 999	48.9	48.0	2.4	0.7
300-999	28.4	60.2	9.2	2.2
100-299	16.5	59.1	18.4	6.0
30-99	10.4	48.4	30.6	10.6
Total	14.7	52.1	24.8	8.4
Technical				
5 000 or more	57.8	39.2	2.5	0.5
1 000-4 999	40.2	53.7	4.2	1.9
300-999	24.1	64.8	7.8	3.3
100-299	15.7	61.2	14.5	8.6
30-99	11.4	46.7	27.8	14.1
Total	14.4	52.1	22.0	11.5
HIGH-SCHOOL GRADUATES				
Clerical				
5 000 or more	54.3	42.5	3.2	–
1 000-4 999	39.0	55.8	4.3	0.9
300-999	22.3	63.7	11.6	2.4
100-299	14.9	59.1	21.5	4.5
30-99	8.0	48.1	34.3	9.6
Total	11.3	51.9	29.1	7.7
Production				
5 000 or more	31.7	60.1	7.1	1.1
1 000-4 999	22.4	66.3	9.1	2.2
300-999	16.5	68.8	11.1	3.6
100-299	12.8	64.3	16.5	6.4
30-99	8.4	52.6	29.6	9.4
Total	10.2	56.7	24.9	8.2

Source: Ministry of Labour (Koyo Kanri Chosa), 1981.

development'' in such a way that continuing professional education is integrated into career patterns consonant with corporate economic strategy. In most countries, the step which remains to be taken is the formulation of a policy within which the higher education institutions find their place and perform missions compatible with their specificities.

Measures taken by the public authorities have stimulated the creation of education and training provision, usually with the requirement that these should rapidly become self-financing.

In the case of Finland, discussions concerning the place of continuing professional education in relation to the other components of continuing education in higher education have been going on for several years. Adult education has been divided between the "Open University", and short- and long-term continuing professional education. Various schools of thought in Finnish society include the "neo-traditionalist" school which rejects any form of continuing education, unless it generates funds for basic research; the "cultural" school which expresses qualified acceptance of long-term and probably degree-oriented continuing education, but condemns short-term education, which it does not consider to be the business of higher education; the "utilitarian" school chiefly supports long-term education, but regards short-term a necessity (see Table 18). The utilitarian approach has given rise to the establishment of extension studies centres. Originally, these were justified by the application and dissemination of research and the creation of networks with the employers. They are now integrated into the missions of higher education.

In the Netherlands, continuing education policies cater for three categories of need of different segments of the population: those under the authority of the Ministry of Education and Science; the unemployed and/or redeployed workers; the employed who in the course of their working life undertake specialised, extended or complementary education and training. In the first two cases, public authorities bear the cost, whereas in the third case funding is, or will be, increasingly private – supplied in the main by companies. To move in this direction, public authorities in the Netherlands rely heavily on

Table 18. **Finland: relationships between different schools of thought and adult higher education**

Types of adult higher education

Schools of thought on education and science policy	Open University	Short-term continuing professional education	Long-term continuing professional education
Neo-traditional	Not a necessary basic university function	Not a university function, except to the extent that it helps attract funds for basic research	Not a university function
Cultural (emphasis placed on culture science relationship)	Wholly endorsed, to provide scientific survivalist knowledge and skills for people	Condemnable, not a university function	Justifiable to a certain extent if research-oriented and not professionally-oriented
Utilitarian	To be endorsed with reservations: *a)* to make use of educational reserves *b)* for equality	Constantly necessary to a certain extent; economic profits to university	Indispensable, transmits the most recent research findings to promote occupational changes

Source: Contribution of Finland, 1991 (p. 53).

negotiation and consensus with the social partners. If the latter desire education which approaches more closely to their needs, they have to commit funds, materials and human resources. This policy goes hand in hand with the introduction of contract teaching.

While the trends towards professionalisation and economic responsiveness are clearly marked, definitional problems persist, and the fundamental questions facing higher education and its institutions are far from being solved. These include: access in higher education; certification of continuing education and occupational skills and competences; funding; curbs on development within institutions of higher education.

Implications for higher education institutions

Access

Admission criteria for continuing professional education for highly-qualified personnel are not traditional (Parry and Wake, 1990). Criteria such as age and drop-out rates vary depending upon the length of the education. In the United Kingdom, for example, the growing influx of adults into continuing higher education coexists with an extremely selective policy governing admissions to initial higher education, even if non-university institutions apply less exacting entry criteria. Financing also determines access criteria. When an individual, or his employer pays, academic criteria (previous education or degree) are disregarded, whereas when the education is publicly funded, these criteria are applied. As the view of continuing education changes from one of a ''second chance'' – implying some compatibility between access to initial and continuing education – to that of a lifelong process, access criteria should change. In France, for example, the authorities are anxious to move, at least to some extent, towards a common core curriculum, while at the same time tailoring certain arrangements to the requirements of an adult clientele (guidance procedures, assistance with individual projects, the drawing up of training contracts, and the recognition and accreditation of acquired skills).

Under different names, long- and short-term courses are found in many Member countries (United Kingdom, Netherlands, Germany, Austria, France, the former Yugoslavia). *Long-term courses* are essentially post-initial education, where admission depends directly on initial formal qualifications. The pursuit of education is facilitated by certain institutional arrangements such as single-subject courses (modules), part-time studies and distance learning. But admission remains strictly governed by academic criteria. *Short-term education* comprises courses, seminars and conferences lasting a few days, and usually paid for by the employer. Here, the problem of access tends to lie in the dissemination of information by occupational sectors or industries.

In the Netherlands, where access criteria vary from one type of education and training to another, access in the private sector is left to the discretion of the organisation which is paying or responsible for providing the education. In the public sector, the situation is more varied, depending on the nature of the continuing education. Admission to post-initial higher education, which is sometimes treated as part of continuing education, is based on previous university degrees, as is part-time education. By contrast, no

Table 19. **Germany: admission requirements for participation in continuing education programmes offered by higher education institutions**

In percentage

Admission requirements	Study courses	Single events
Work experience	63	50
Degree in higher education	59[a]	38
Aptitude test	21	4

a) This high percentage may be attributable to the fact that the HIS survey includes high-level university courses, which can be taken by employed persons.
Source: HIS, 1989.

university degrees are required for post-initial continuing education. Each institution demands this or that proof of competence, but there is no systematic approach. Similarly, enrolment in the Open University is not subject to any academic requirements.

In the former Yugoslavia, continuing professional education of highly-qualified personnel consists of the sector for doctorates (for at least two years), and of specialist courses (lasting a year). Access is very strictly linked to traditional academic criteria. The content of short-term upgrading courses (lasting from two weeks to a month) is linked to the occupational environment, and the final qualifications acquired are not academic. Access criteria are less rigid. Several examples are mentioned of continuing professional education set up within the framework of international collaboration, notably with the Netherlands.

In Germany, continuing education is open to those with the essential "aptitudes" to take a given course acquired through employment or elsewhere; prior degrees are not required. Criteria evaluation is the responsibility of the institution of higher education and these vary considerably depending on whether "study courses" (long-term) or "single events" (short-term) are concerned. In the former case, an initial higher education degree continues to carry considerable weight, even though professional experience remains the primary criterion. In the case of "single events", the degree has less significance (Table 19).

Italy is an exception, being particularly attached to academic recognition of competence. The survey carried out as part of the Italian contribution, and relating to the private system, shows that admission criteria are still strongly linked to a university degree or to extended secondary education, to which a demand for professional experience is increasingly often added.

Certification

Recognising and certifying acquired knowledge and competences continues to be one of the major problems confronting continuing education and institutions of higher education. These are the only institutions to award socially and professionally recognised degrees and diplomas, but they do not traditionally consult external authorities, whether ministries, employers or commissions (exceptions at the time were the British Polytechnics and Colleges). Institutions of higher education evaluate academic knowledge within precisely defined disciplines: experience, skills, and competences acquired prior to or after education alter the fundamental notion of certification. But there is a real economic and professional need for another form of certification linking academic knowledge to work experience, and the issues are more sweeping than simply harmonizing degrees between the institutions of a single country or among several Member countries. The need for new forms of certification, together with the rise of education and training in the formal and non-formal sectors, will create pressure for change. Certificates will become "transferable", or "portable" from one work situation to another, from an academic to a professional post, and *vice versa,* and new elements will be added to the previous evaluation schemes such as advancement over time, learning performed in different places, and the individualisation of learning geared to employment and career development.

For example, the extent to which education, training and certification are fundamental issues in joint agreements and collective bargaining (Madigan, 1990) varies by country. The quality of the link may explain why continuing education does not enjoy any recognised professional status, and why competences acquired often at the cost of great individual effort and a substantial financial investment receive less social and professional recognition than does initial higher education.

The status of continuing education is an important issue here because highly-qualified personnel are not all products of initial higher education and various Member countries mention it as a curb to its development. The Yugoslav contribution, for instance, expands on the problem created by the negative attitude to non-degree continuing professional education which has no status on the labour market or in the enterprise.

This tension has real national economic, social, educational repercussions. A continuing education degree is discernibly appealing in several countries where the social and professional standing of certification is still extremely powerful and constitutes a minimum formal requirement for entry into many jobs (France, Finland).

The Finnish situation illustrates an extreme position inasmuch as initial higher education is gradually acquiring merely intermediate status. Developments in continuing education have given rise to new certificates whose value relative to the traditional degrees is not yet established, but which have already acquired "practical recognition" on the labour market. However, the tradition of the labour market is so rigid that a certificate of continuing education, even if it enjoys high practical recognition, needs to be backed up by a degree or diploma concordant with the classical academic symbols.

By contrast, in Norway there is no traditional link between certification and salary level. Two criteria are important for professional advancement: first, the acquisition of professional competence (measured in terms of economic viability from the corporate standpoint); second, seniority (particularly in the civil service). Salary is dictated by the hierarchy and not by certification. Access to continuing in-house training and external continuing professional education is guided by "employee talks", during which education and training needs are assessed, and training is more or less guaranteed. This practice is fairly general in large corporations, and enables an individual response to be made to training and recognition matters. Within the ministry, a National Co-ordinating Committee (NKU) lists and approves examinations organised outside the public-sector institutions, and assesses their equivalence to university and college examinations in credits. This approval is sought by private colleges including distance education, but not by the commercial sector which seldom uses examinations. In the last years both employers and employees are more concerned about getting professional continuing education certified as a quality guarantee.

Certification is a necessary subject of debate which, however, seems to arouse sharply conflicting interests. On the one hand, there is the vital guarantee for the employee and, on the other, the risk for the employers of improved qualifications leading to increased mobility. As the employer develops in-house training markets that open up career opportunities, large corporations are intervening increasingly in formal educational processes at secondary and tertiary levels.

Increasingly, both the social and economic partners and the public authorities are deliberating on the possibility of recognising "real" skills and competences, defined as those acquired by individuals in their professional, social and cultural life, outside the formal education system. In Norway in 1986, for example, the Commission on Lifelong Learning inserted this question into the government's 1988/89 White Paper. Similarly, in Japan, a high-level expert committee on the education and training of engineers was set up in 1990 under the aegis of the Ministry of Education, Science and Culture. Another committee was formed the same year at the instigation of the Ministry of Labour to examine the continuing education of highly-qualified personnel. In an increasing number of countries we find both traditions and more or less innovative experiments in certification, ranging from certificates of attendance to the recognition of experientially-acquired knowledge, skills and competences. The expansion of continuing education and continuing professional education demands that we consider the social and professional recognition of professional, experiential skills acquired without creating a two-tiered education system – the one esteemed because it is based on initial higher education and the other less prestigious because it is based on continuing education.

Certificate of attendance (Italy, the Netherlands)

Certificates of attendance seem to be by far the most widespread, and are at any rate the easiest to adopt. In private-sector training establishments in Italy, for instance, certification usually takes the form of a certificate of attendance. In the public sector, certificates of qualification (for the unemployed receiving training) and certificates of attendance are the two most usual forms of recognition. In the Netherlands, only training for doctorates and the training of teachers are subject to national regulations. For all other training, institutions of post-initial higher education award certificates of attendance for education and training courses.

Credit units (Germany, Austria, Norway, Sweden)

Sweden is a typical example of the co-ordination between continuing and initial education; Germany and Austria are currently considering the expediency of such a link. At the moment, a certificate of attendance most often attests to participation in continuing professional education, which signifies that the student has been present at 70 per cent of the programme. On rare occasions, the certificate mentions course content and results. How are results integrated into the "qualifications scale"? The February 1990 resolution by the Commission for Educational Planning and Research Promotion *(Ausschuss Bildungsplanung der Bundesländer,* BKL) lays down that the certificate awarded after continuing education should state the levels of competence, programme contents, scope and evaluation procedures used. In the long term, such a resolution leads the labour market to recognise the skills and/or competence attained in continuing education and opens the possibility of integrating them into the framework of initial higher education by means of a credit unit (credit points).

In Austria, the criteria governing professional advancement are essentially linked to initial higher education diplomas/degrees (at secondary and university levels). Individuals are therefore not encouraged to take part in continuing education which has no impact on their professional status. They prefer to develop very long initial education strategies, whose results will be recognised, and to ignore continuing education. A credit unit system has been proposed in both these countries which would oblige initial education to recognise knowledge acquired in continuing education and to integrate it into the initial education. Greater flexibility and the implementation of, and participation in, a continuing adult education policy should follow.

Recognising skills

The United Kingdom, France, the United States, Norway and Australia are moving towards recognising non-academic knowledge. In general, there are increasingly close links between the institutions of higher education, professional associations, and the economic and social partners. This issue is relatively recent in higher education and, more generally, in advanced education and training, although it has long been raised and practiced in initial and continuing secondary education (OECD, 1990*e*; Slowey, 1991). While the question of harmonizing certificates remains important, it is restricted to institutions of higher education. The issue here is entirely different and requires examining recognition and accreditation of general and vocational expertise acquired outside academic studies, in continuing education and/or social, cultural and professional experience. Recent innovative attempts to recognise and accredit professional competences focus on professional tasks, training institutions and individuals (professional competence). These practices affect higher education, continuing education and labour market policies, and require that each evaluates the benefits of the new proposed collaborations or changes of traditional practices or missions.

Innovations

In the United Kingdom, professional associations are tending to move away gradually from managing their own examination systems towards a position of greater confidence in educational institutions. In most cases, these associations are keen on maintaining skills and competences as well as their accreditation, even though they may not have specially demanded certification as a means of quality assurance. A survey carried out in the United Kingdom in 1989 (Welsh and Woodward, 1990) involving 1.4 million professionals (123 associations out of the 240 contacted, excluding doctors and teachers) shows the importance of evaluation upon entry into the profession. The results show that 47 per cent of the associations which replied had laid down a continuing professional education policy, and that 30 per cent were thinking of doing so. The policies vary considerably. Generally speaking, it is up to the individual to undertake education and training, in accordance with the scheme suggested by the association. Forty-four per cent of associations use the concept of the "portfolio", reflecting the impact of the Engineering Council.

In higher education in the United Kingdom, polytechnics, considered the most innovative institutions for long-term education, are the most active in trying out new systems of certification targeting occupational-vocational courses which are not exclusively academic. The Woolwich Building Society and Thames Polytechnic, for example, are offering a first degree which includes performance evaluation based either on interviews with a senior professional or on an annual professional evaluation system. Many "Masters" courses have been set up in conjunction with enterprises. Similar collaborative experiments are being conducted with industry in order to establish custom-designed programmes arranged on a modular basis. Higher education is offering experience and certification to continuing education by making major efforts to improve flexibility without sacrificing quality.

In France, there are various forms of certification: national diplomas, individual institutional diplomas, and certificates of attendance. National diplomas facilitate entry to the labour market because they are widely recognised, and are used as standards in collective agreements. Diplomas from individual institutions are sanctioned by the Commission d'homologation des titres et diplômes (Degree and Diploma Approvals Board) in order to guarantee quality. Certificates of attendance are the direct responsibility of the training agencies. Since 1974, the rules and regulations have been revised to facilitate access to education and diplomas for the employed: the *Examen spécial d'accès aux études universitaires* (ESEU – Special University Entrance Examination) lets those without baccalauréats enter a university, while the 1985 Decree deals with the accreditation of acquired skills and lets institutions accredit professional experience, knowledge or individual aptitudes acquired outside any formal system of education or training. Little use has so far been made of this facility. Short-term courses (distinct from long-term courses arranged in modules) raise different problems because they do not generally evaluate or recognise knowledge, skills and competences acquired.

Recognising professional skills

In 1986, a working party set up by the Manpower Services Commission and the Department of Education and Science in the United Kingdom published a report on the restructuring of vocational qualifications recommending that applied skills and abilities, wider opportunities for professional advancement, and the certification of education, training and work in integrated programmes be recognised. The National Council for Vocational Qualifications (NCVQ) was assigned the task of assessing and rationalising evaluation procedures at all levels of the education system and put forward the most carefully worked out system. The approach is based on recognising professional skills needed to carry out tasks predetermined by a job analysis, taking into account the professional context. Against this backdrop, some professions are concerned about reduced recognition for academic knowledge. Many university staff and employers voice doubts about the credibility of the evaluators, whereas academic peer-group assessments are well established. The efforts of the Management Charter Initiative make clear how delicate these questions are because they impinge on the often divergent interests of professional associations and higher education institutions. Thus, the project, supported by some 200 employers, to establish a Management MBA based on recognition of professional skills and competences had to be abandoned.

Recognising training institutions

The German and Austrian "credits" schemes have to be considered in the context of this approach, the subject of many developments in the Council for National Academic Awards (CNAA) in the United Kingdom, whose principal role was to recognise degrees awarded by polytechnics and colleges and which thereby approves one-third of the degrees awarded in the United Kingdom. The general idea behind the proposal, which has been debated by the CNAA since 1987, is that professional and academic knowledge, skills and competences should be eligible for certification and should count towards, for example, a professional master's degree. Thus, company training could be mixed with academic knowledge.

The Credit Accumulation and Transfer Scheme (CATS), set up in 1986, provides a special service for students, employers, professional associations, and educational institutions by facilitating adult access to higher education. Prior professional or academic experience can be recognised by CATS, and students can apply this recognition in future studies. Professional associations can make use of CATS to extend their continuing professional education opportunities. This system encourages higher education institutions to open their doors to young and mature non-traditional students, and to legitimise different forms of learning. Currently, thirty "consortia" of educational institutions offer facilities for the recognition of continuing education under the CATS scheme.

A similar approach is currently being examined in Japan where the attitude towards certification is that professional requirements can be met by an infinity of skills rather than a previously determined and standardized range of skills. The Japanese approach envisages the flexible application of skills in response to the developmental potential of job content. The Ministry of Labour has convened a high-level group of experts to consider the expediency of creating a master's qualification based on a system of units.

The proposal should allow candidates to take courses in various institutions – universities or Special Training Schools. The Manpower Development Organisation would approve the courses, which would count for an equivalent number of basic units towards the "master's" qualification. At the end of the training process, the candidate would be awarded a legally recognised "master's" certificate, whose status, however, would be different from that of the master's degree awarded by initial higher education. There was to be an initial trial in mid-1990 in accountancy to serve as a foundation for more extensive changes in the methods of attesting knowledge, skills and competences.

This Japanese initiative is supported by a tradition in which qualifications are recognised by a public system of certification. Traditionally, examinations necessary for degrees do not legally require preparation in a teaching institution. The public certification system is therefore to some extent accustomed to recognising knowledge gained from experience, in addition to initial or continuing education. On the other hand, the emphasis placed on individual responsibility in continuing professional education, and the development of some mobility, make it vital for individuals, employers and the public authorities that knowledge, skills and competences acquired by various means (work, formal education, in-house training) be certificated.

Recognising individuals' qualities

Recognition centred on the individual, the subject of many experiments and much research, raises the question of vocational and social context. The French experience of "Assessment Centres" highlights this issue. In Manchester in 1988, for example, five institutions of higher education set up CONTACT – the Consortium for Advanced Continuing Education and Training – to clarify education and training goals, and provision directly linked to occupational objectives. CONTACT offers a Continuing Professional Development Award (CPDA), a certificate attesting that professional competence has been updated and developed. Certification demands 120 hours of training. The design of CPDA courses reflects the needs and concerns of professionals in the workplace. Additionally, some of the units obtained in this way also count towards a degree.

This form of recognition confirms mastery of a restricted range of knowledge relating to a single subject. It is interesting to note in this experiment that while new acquisitions are not necessarily coherent in academic or professional terms, they are linked to individual needs, previous experience and professional requirements. Currently, 7 per cent of the higher education institutions in the United Kingdom subscribe to this system which is arousing great interest among employers and professional associations who wish to see their training recognised by CONTACT certificates.

Funding

The dynamic of the relationship between higher education and the economic environment revives the question of the present balance between public, individual, and industry funds. Mixed funding is on the increase, while the individual burden is liable to grow (Netherlands, United Kingdom, United States). The coherence of national policies must be re-examined. In the various Member countries, the funding policies for continuing professional education are clear, and demand a real-cost basis without help from the taxpayer or fiscal support. Public sector participation distinguishes adult education (recurrent education, second chance) from that considered in this report, which, more than any other area of adult education, is destined to be self-financed.

National funding policies demanding true-cost unsubsidised continuing professional education remain largely theoretical partly because training is not yet a sufficiently pressing issue and individuals are not encouraged to commit themselves. This point has important consequences given that most professional associations are putting forward continuing professional education policies based on individual responsibility. On the other hand, taxation policy is not always equitable. In the United Kingdom, training organisations have to pay VAT on the training services they sell, whereas higher education institutions and some professional associations are exempted. There is therefore a frequently expressed desire for parity among providers.

In Norway, the cost of continuing professional education based on improved performance in the current job is tax-deductible, whereas the generally more expensive employee-borne cost for continuing professional education for a job change into more highly-skilled employment is not deductible. In fact, there are three basic situations:

a) virtually all funding is public (Germany, Austria);
b) short-term education is self-financing (United States, France), or should fairly quickly become self-financing (United Kingdom, Italy, Netherlands);
c) A self-financing system is integrated into the government-funded higher education system (Sweden).

Public funding of continuing professional education

In Germany, initial higher education is state-funded. Since 1976, continuing education, which is one of the missions of higher education institutions, is massively funded from the same source. This means, particularly where long-term "study courses" are concerned, that the participants contribute only 21 per cent, while nearly 58 per cent of the funds come out of the budget of the institutions of higher education (Table 20). In the

Table 20. **Germany: proportion of different sources for financing continuing education programmes offered by higher education institutions**

In percentage

Sources	Study courses	Single events
Participants' fees	21	41
Budget of higher education institutions	58	40
Other state funds	10	7
Funds of third parties	7	9
Other funds	4	3

Source: HIS, 1989.

more expensive occupational short-term single events", employers bear the major share of the financial burden (41 per cent). This situation, which has prevailed for over 15 years, reflects the practical state of affairs, and expresses neither a consensus nor the philosophy behind the 1976 Framework Act on Higher Education.

In both Germany and Austria, the issue today is that by charging fees at a very modest level, institutions do not compete in a market economy. Other providers are obliged to charge real-cost-based fees; professors therefore support continuing education pursued outside the university as a rewarding source of income. It follows that the institutions must become more cost-conscious in order for continuing education to develop within, rather than outside, higher education.

Public authorities are planning the adoption in the near future of funding mechanisms identical to those which have been in operation for several years in the other OECD countries.

Countries point out that the continuing education of "disadvantaged" adults conforms to different funding rules and procedures. Finland provides an example of a financial aid system which is totally separate from that for continuing professional education and extremely advantageous to "mature students". Under this scheme it is possible for those over 25 with over five years of work experience, and/or for those without a degree, to obtain aid equal to 122 per cent of their net pay.

In the Netherlands, explicit rules govern funding directly linked to ministerial responsibility for the facilities concerned. Officially, two cases are possible:

a) the ministry is the principal employer, as is the case with teachers, or directly responsible for the profession in question, as with researchers, and bears responsibility for the continuing training system. In addition, part-time education and the Open University are State-funded under the heading of initial higher education;

b) clients for education and training services are not dependent on the ministry, which bears no responsibility for funding training aimed at improving the quality of service in a given occupation. Employers pay.

Self-funding policies for short-term education

Although the national context differs, France provides another good example of the difficulties of defining indicators and of financial complexities. Higher education accounts for some 5 per cent of the total number of trainees and trainee-hours, but receives only 2 per cent of the total training budget. Physical indicators give a bigger figure for higher education than the financial indicators because per-trainee cost is relatively lower. They often do not include any depreciation on the buildings or for specialised research laboratory equipment because they have been publicly financed under a different heading. In private sector funding in particular, there is a wide gap between the physical indicators (7.5 per cent of trainees and 7.3 per cent of trainee-hours) and the financial indicator (2.3 per cent) due partly to the comparatively low average per-hour cost of training in institutions of higher education but mainly to the comparatively high per-trainee cost in the corporate sector itself, due to the fact that all operating and, more particularly, capital costs are counted in training outlays. More generally, practices such as these raise the question of what proportion of continuing professional education is financed by the government.

At the moment, enterprises are more heavily engaged in dialogue with higher education. Industry is the main source of finance for short-term education, and for long-term education undertaken in collaboration with the higher education institution. Most often, the partners are large corporations who have an eye to their own strategic development.

In the United Kingdom, the clearest policy relates to short-term education. The cost-price rules apply, and competition operates effectively. This reality affects the whole range of higher education, and most immediately the non-university sector. However, the higher education institutions have made extensive use of the funds available through such agencies as the National Advisory Body for Public Sector Higher Education (NAB), which has now become the Polytechnics and Colleges Funding Council (PCFC), and the University Grants Committee (UGC), now the Universities Funding Council (UFC), to expand their short- and long-term education services with substantial government support.

In the Netherlands, government funding for education and training activities outside the area of ministerial responsibility is restricted to start-up grants within a short-term time frame. Up to 1991 the government allocated a certain amount of financial support to higher-level continuing education, which had then to become financially self-supporting.

Integrating self-funded short-term education into publicly funded higher education?

In the Swedish system, it is very difficult to distinguish initial education and continuing education, and even more difficult to differentiate continuing education from continuing professional education. To get round this difficulty, the country contribution examined the role of the employers in providing funds for education and training, which allows the volume of continuing professional education to be assessed. It does not mean that this training targets highly-qualified personnel, but it does indicate the trend towards professionalisation.

In this "integrated system", the same course may be taken by students funded by different mechanisms, and the financial criterion seems to be the only way of differentiating those in initial education from those in continuing education. But this criterion does not operate systematically: students in initial education may owe their presence to personnel education, paid for by their employer, or to commissioned education, and they may be taking the same courses as students receiving initial higher education.

General resource restrictions have favoured the development of "commissioned education" which has enabled higher education institutions to recruit staff. These activities allow smaller higher education institutions to extend their operations beyond the limits set by government funds. Major universities react differently. The perceived advantages relate to links with the world of work, which offer university professors opportunities for contacts. However, critics point out that "commissioned education" is aimed at those able to pay for training facilities, while – seen from another legislative standpoint – access to such training presupposes competition. During the 1980s, "commissioned education" grew rapidly in the institutions of higher education, but in 1989 and 1990 the trend has slackened off.

Curbs on development

The country contributions focus on several curbs on development: the attachment to traditional academic values, the relatively weak advance of traditions of continuing education in national economic fabrics, and the status of the teaching staff for whom continuing education does not benefit their careers.

Attachment to traditional academic values

The German and Austrian situations illustrate the problem of the poor co-ordination of continuing education and institutional missions. Since 1976, continuing education has been ranked as a full-fledged university mission, despite its modest presence. It is publicly funded, which paradoxically thwarts its growth because teaching staff prefer the extra income of teaching outside the university. Moreover, the co-presence of continuing education absorbs a substantial portion of university budgets for initial education and research, and to some extent subsidises continuing education of highly-qualified personnel. To different degrees, this same problem exists in the United Kingdom, France, Japan and the former Yugoslavia.

Weak tradition of continuing education

The situation in the United Kingdom illustrates the problem of the weak tradition of continuing education, and its unenthusiastic reception in academic circles as well as in industrial and professional quarters with their own traditions. Despite progress in discussion, the focal point has to be the creation of a training system responsive to professional requirements and active in preparing for changes. In order to promote an industrial culture with regular recourse to continuing education, the question arises of fiscally regulating the situation through business and personal taxes.

The status of teaching staff

The reluctance of teaching staff, for whom continuing education does not benefit their career path (United Kingdom, France, Germany, Austria), is primarily for financial reasons. For example, in Germany 70 per cent of professors may teach up to 80 hours per year outside their institutions (1989 HIS survey). To ascertain the extent of the phenomenon, the Austrian Institute of Educational Research for the Economy *(Institut für Bildungsforschung der Wirtschaft)* has carried out a survey to estimate the involvement of teaching staff in continuing education activities outside the university. It covers a large number of continuing education agencies of importance in the national context: chambers of commerce, schools, management institutes, corporate training centres, establishments providing general education services, and civil service training centres. Of the 150 enterprises contacted, 55 (representing approximately 225 000 employees) replied. Although

Table 21. **Austria: continuing education provided by university professors outside of universities, by discipline**

In percentage

Disciplines	Enterprises	Training Institutions
Management and business administration	56	41
Engineering	23	24
Social sciences and humanities	13	14
Law	4	17
Unknown	4	4

Source: Austrian Economic Institute of Research in Education, 1990.

this is not an exhaustive survey, it does have the merit of providing an initial picture of a phenomenon to which attention has been widely drawn in the Member countries, and which is still difficult to gauge.

The results show that it is usually enterprises which have recourse to university teachers. Sixteen per cent of their teachers come from the universities, whereas only 2 per cent of those employed in educational institutes are drawn from university teaching staff. Note must, however, be taken of management institutes, in which 10-15 per cent of the staff come from the universities. It is interesting to observe the disciplines for which university teachers are called (Table 21). Both enterprises and educational institutes concentrate on teachers of "business and administration". Noticeable is the modest role of teachers of law, especially in enterprises.

The Finnish situation throws an interesting light on the modified status of teaching staff. The extension studies centres are institutions under the authority of the central university administration, in the same way, say, as a university library, language centre or computer centre. Under their rules, there is no permanent teaching establishment, and this factor is regarded as vital to their success. Professors and experts are engaged for particular educational programmes, and the choice is restricted to those with a high level of expertise in science and pedagogy. It is also interesting to note the reasons given by teachers for engaging in continuing education activities in addition to their ordinary course work. The first reason quoted is that of additional earnings, followed by considerations relating to teaching (teaching adults is more rewarding than teaching the young), and putting their scientific theories to the test. According to the Finnish contribution, the last consideration applies to teachers of the humanities and social sciences.

The roles of higher education in the training market

Three questions were put to those responsible for education, in an effort to identify national missions in each Member country; they summarise three choices:

i) Should the roles of the formal sector – university and non-university higher education – be limited?

ii) Should the roles of the formal sector be redefined within a broader framework for higher education (or higher education and training)?

iii) Should new means be provided for interaction with the labour market? If so, how should they be provided?

If institutions of higher education wish to maintain their excellence and effectiveness while managing an increasingly diversified education system linked to the economic, social and cultural environment, they face a permanent challenge. They have an as yet unexploited capacity for creating multidisciplinary and/or research-linked continuing education facilities, but they cannot indefinitely redefine and expand their missions. Nor can they compete with commercial and professional providers. Even if higher education has diversified the institutions in which training is dispensed to include training in the non-formal and commercial sectors, and widened the very concept of higher education (Schuller, 1991), it should remain committed to setting up education and training in areas within its sphere of competence rather than attempting to be comprehensive, or providing programmes offered by other private or public institutions that compete in a free market. The question of the functions which can be usefully assumed by public authorities and by those responsible for other educational sectors is important (Van Vught, 1989).

During the 1970s and 1980s, attempts to co-ordinate education, training, and employment manifestly failed. Experiments in secondary and post-secondary education, where attention to the labour-education relationship is greater than in higher education, give clear examples. The labour market did not know what signals to send, forecasts were unreliable and those in education did not know how to read the signals. In sum, we would ask how a new dynamic can be developed for the coming decade, capable of accommodating the missions of higher education. As it faces the same problem, how can higher education remain responsive to and anticipatory of changing job requirements? The Netherlands offers an interesting example. Public authorities try to determine a consensual policy on future directions and missions of higher education, while at the same time seeking to maintain a clear picture of the responsibilities specific to each partner. Institutional responsibilities must be accepted and pursued in creating mechanisms favourable to interaction with the labour market. Such a policy orientation raises the delicate question of balancing co-operation and, eventually, suppression of competition.

Chapter IV

Five Challenges for the Future

Diversified demand and targeted supply

The market for adult education in general and for higher continuing professional education in particular will grow in the coming years, although by how much cannot be predetermined. Growth will be due to demographic changes, to changing notions of knowledge and skills (their acquisition, their obsolescence and their renewal) and to their consequences for the traditional roles and capacity of the formal and non-formal institutions of higher education, professional associations and in-house company training as well as the emerging commercial sector. No single "provider" will be able to cope with such a range of demands. That is why the approach adopted here has been to compare the different providers, each of which plays a specific and evolving role.

Training for the private sector without losing specificities

The relationship between higher education and the labour market is fairly positive, but many important difficulties remain which are fundamental for the development of the enterprises and economies of the Member countries. As the market for continuing education for highly-qualified personnel broadens to include, increasingly, institutions of higher education, their traditional missions must be reconsidered while their unique role of providing initial higher education and research is preserved. Internal management issues ranging from teaching and research staff roles to course content will emerge as a result of this evolution, as well as changes in student definition, access, training, and certification. Institutional as well as national policies need to be formulated to meet these challenges.

Competition and the market

The different sectors do not enjoy a completely unregulated dynamic relationship. It is therefore difficult to speak of a continuing professional education market in the full sense of the term in which the forces of supply and demand are in free play. Fundamental obstacles to free-market competition include the traditionally non-economic funding of higher education, and the virtual domination of certain sectors. France notes that the non-formal market, controlled by the corporate sector, is so large that the genuinely free market in which agreements are drawn up directly between training agencies and the customer, is only residual. This sector is expanding as the market tends to split into comparatively watertight segments, in some of which higher education institutions are finding it difficult to establish a foothold. They may react, however, to the demand by adopting commercial criteria (Sweden, Finland, United Kingdom, Netherlands, France) (Bordage, 1992).

In general, relations being established between the formal and non-formal sectors tend towards collaboration. Similarly, professional associations seek collaboration with the institutions of higher education chiefly in order to ensure their members' access to recognised, good-quality education and training.

The commercial sector is the most responsive. The education it offers is based on real costs and, not being hindered by institutional inertial, can respond quickly to demands. Thus, this sector may be called upon to fill gaps left open by the formal sector, which, however, expresses scepticism about the quality of training that it offers.

It is time to examine national continuing professional education strategies, and to incorporate them in higher education policies. These policies would, of course, consider national contexts and return to the question of information availability and data collection for analysis.

Co-ordinating initial and continuing education

As Squires (1993) has observed, co-ordination between initial higher education and continuing education can follow one of two courses: the initial education is long and thorough or shorter and specialised. In the first case, initial education could produce graduates thoroughly trained in their particular discipline and fully conversant with the latest developments in it. Here, there is little room for "non-technical", more general and peripheral subjects. Professional experience will make continuing professional education in the humanities and social sciences more valuable.

Thus, as mentioned in the German study, continuing professional education and continuing education in general could help to reduce the length of initial higher education. The curriculum would define basic knowledge within the "propedeutic semesters" and a catalogue of optional specialisations for the students in the following semesters. After graduation and some years of working experience, short periods of continuing education could usefully cater for special experiences and further qualification needs. This option raises the questions of costs and leave of absence from employment.

In the second case, initial education produces a less technically accomplished but more adaptable graduate who is able to appreciate variety, contextual diversity and unforeseeable changes into work organisation. Here, continuing professional education would give graduates supplementary, specialised training. This approach assumes that: technological advance makes it difficult to keep initial education current in all areas;

education and training in all spearhead technologies cannot be offered; many graduates make more use in their professional lives of their general expertise than their specialised technical knowledge.

The choice of one or the other course will affect the length and content of initial education, the temporal balance between a general and a specialised education, recognition of initial degrees and continuing professional education and the balance between the professional, social and cultural experiences of an individual. No single model, however, can meet all employers' needs.

Initiating a new social dialogue

A comprehensive review of the whole range of higher education and training provided by institutions of higher education, enterprises, professional associations and the commercial sector must be undertaken. Country contributions clearly state that the demand is difficult to evaluate for want of information. The same is true about costs. Implementing a new approach calls for a more intensive dialogue between the actors, without necessarily reaching a consensus, so that they can put together a coherent education and training system (Commission of European Communities, 1991).

The task for the public authorities (ministries and regional authorities) is to redefine the thrust of higher education and the missions of continuing education. The partners involved in the continuing professional education market can then discuss the major educational choices, and the direction to be taken by higher education and higher training levels. As the country contributions point out, it is essential to bring these partners together so that they can proceed in the same direction. An overall pattern compatible with particular national economic, social and cultural features needs to be drawn in order to best delineate the mission and potential for continuing professional education.

Annex 1

Statistical Information

Table A.1. **Participation rate: third-level education, 1986**

	Percentage
Austria	27
Belgium	32
Canada	53
Denmark	28
Finland	36
France	30
Germany	29
Greece	27
Ireland	26
Italy	24
Japan	30
Netherlands	36
New Zealand	36
Norway	32
Spain	30
Sweden	30
Switzerland	22
Turkey	10
United Kingdom	22
United States	60
Yugoslavia	19

Source: Education in OECD Countries, 1987-88, OECD, Paris, 1990.

Table A.2. **Percentage of the population having at least some post-secondary education, by sex, 1988**

	Level D[a]		Level E[b]	
	Males	Females	Males	Females
Australia	11.1	23.7	9.6	5.5
Austria			6.2	3.5
Belgium			14.6	12.0
Canada	21.8	23.3	14.1	10.3
Finland			11.0	9.6
Germany	3.9	1.2	6.0	3.2
Italy			5.5	3.7
Japan	5.3	11.6	18.9	4.4
Netherlands	14.1	10.2	6.1	1.9
Norway			19.5	15.8
Portugal	0.8	2.5	3.4	2.0
Spain	4.3	4.5	4.1	2.1
Sweden	9.8	11.3	11.5	10.2
Switzerland	5.9	2.3	13.8	11.6
United Kingdom			16.6	14.8
United States	18.4	19.0	22.4	16.3

a) Level D: partial post-secondary studies not sanctioned by a university degree.
b) Level E: studies sanctioned by at least one university degree.
Source: Employment Outlook, July 1989, OECD, Paris (excerpt from Table 2.1).

Table A.3. **France: higher education's penetration of the market for continuing professional education in terms of funding and number of trainees, 1989**

In percentage

	Funding assigned to higher education for continuing professional education	Participants in higher education as a proportion of the total continuing professional education
Private funding	2.3	7.5
Public funding	1.5	3.4
Total	1.9	5.4

Source: French contribution, 1992 (pp. 47 and 48).

Table A.4. **France: breakdown of the funding for providers of continuing professional education, 1989**

	FF billions	Percentage
Min. of Education institutions[a]	7.3	16.0
Other ministries	0.3	0.7
Apprentice training centres[b]	3.6	7.9
Association pour la formation professionnelle des adultes[c]	3.9	8.6
In-house training centres of government administrations	7.4	16.4
Corporate sector training centres	5.6	12.3
Private non-profit organisations[d]	9.3	20.5
Institutions run by business associations	1.7	3.8
Commercial organisations (profit-making)	6.3	13.8
Total	45.4	100.0

a) Figures refer to secondary schools which have pooled their resources in order to set up "Group Schools" (GRETA – Groupements d'établissements) and higher education institutions; they cover continuing education and training programmes provided by special services and agencies belonging to the Ministry of Education, but exclude training provided for its own staff.
b) Alternate in-school/enterprise-based training organised by business associations in conjunction with the Ministry of Education and, since 1983, financed by the regions.
c) AFPA, semi-public organisation linked to the Ministry of Labour, Employment and Vocational Training.
d) This comprises the associative sector, mainly the *Associations d'éducation populaire*.
Source: French contribution, 1992.

Table A.5. **France: breakdown of the training market by different types of provider, 1988**

In percentage

Providers	Number of trainees	%	Trainee-hours (millions)	%	Funding (millions F)	%
Associations 1901 act (ASFO, AFPA, other)	75 000	26.8	42.8	40.0	570.6	13.9
Various types of company incorporated under private law (SA, SARL, etc.)	1 400	0.5	0.9	0.8	1.2	0.9
Other private law agencies (trade associations, mutual associations, social security organisations, etc.)	3 640	1.3	1.5	1.4	21.9	1.3
Total private providers	80 040	28.6	45.2	42.2	607.7	36.1
Ministry of Education Institutions (total)	123 410	44.1	36.9	34.4	668.2	39.7
Secondary-level institutions	69 400	24.8	23.34	21.7	430.9	25.6
Universities	27 420	9.8	10.4	9.7	178.4	10.6
CNAM	26 030	9.3	2.9	2.7	50.5	3.0
Others	560	0.2	0.3	0.3	8.4	0.5
Institutions belonging to other Ministries (Health, Agriculture, etc.)	24 070	8.6	11.9	11.1	198.6	11.8
Business associations and allied training centres (CCI, Chambers of Agriculture and Trades)	49 240	17.6	12.1	11.3	193.7	11.5
Other public law agencies	3 080	1.1	1.1	1.0	15.2	0.9
Total public providers	199 800	71.4	62.0	57.8	1 075.7	63.9
Grand total	279 840	100.0	107.2	100.0	1.683.4	100.0

Source: DFP, Projet de Loi de Finances pour 1990, Document annexe, Formation Professionnelle.

Table A.6. **Sweden: adult education providers, 1989**

Gainfully employed persons taking part in personnel education during 1989 (converted into whole-year equivalents) per education provider

Education provider	Whole-year equivalents (1 year) %	Participants in Spring 1989 (1/2 year) (thousands)
Own employer	64	931
Other company	7	139
University/college	10	33
Other providers	8	110
Municipal adult education (KOMVUX)	3	10
Trade unions	2	42
Adult education associations	1	28
Employment training (AMU)	1	9
Provider unknown	4	123
Total: whole-year equivalent		
Per cent	100	
Number	98 900	1 425

Source: Statistics Sweden, Sweden contribution, 1991.

Table A.7. **United Kingdom: survey of employers:**[a] **training provided by the external training providers, 1987/88**

	University	Poly/IHE	College of Further Education (CFE)	Skills training agency	Industry sector body	Private provider
Weighted base (all establishments excluding London)	28	85	174	125	144	199
Sample size (employers)	33	118	181	111	146	188
			Main answers (percentages)			
Further/higher education courses	34	22	17	2	2	2
Teaching professional skills	10	12	13	2	3	1
Manager supervisory training	30	7	13	20	13	–

a) Employers were asked:
   i) what providers do you use most?
   ii) Can you provide the type of training they provide for your staff? Neither question was pre-coded.
Source: Training Agency, 1989i; *Training in Britain: Market Perspectives*, Her Majesty's Stationary Office, London.

Table A.8. **United Kingdom: number of training days by providers, 1986/87**

Providers	Number of days training (millions)	%
Employers (in-house)[a]	115	33
Private organisations	15	4
Post-compulsory[b] education		
Public[c]	170	49
Universities[d]	50	14
Total	350	100

a) Employers financed roughly 145 million training days, of which some 30 million were provided by the education sector or by private organisations.
b) Excluding schools. It is estimated that in 1986/87 about 95 million training days were provided in schools to students aged 16 and over.
c) Including polytechnics and colleges of higher education, colleges of further education and associated institutions, tertiary colleges and adult education centres.
d) Including Open University courses.
Sources: *Training in Britain: Employer's activities; Training in Britain: Private providers;* DES statistics; FETA report, 1990 (p. 3).

Table A.9. **United States: evolution in the providers' market shares in adult education, 1975 to 1984**
In percentage

Providers	1975	1978	1981	1984
Higher education sector	39	33	31	26
Non-higher education sector	18	16	15	15
Private sector	22	31	38	43
Private communities organisations	8	7	7	7
Government agency	6	7	6	6
Not reported	6	6	3	3

Source: *Trends in Adult Education 1969-1984*. Office of Educational Research and Improvement, US Department of Education, 1985.

Annex 2

National Contributions

Australia

Richard Johnson and Geoffrey Caldwell, Centre for Continuing Education, Australian National University, 1992.

Austria

Elsa Hackl, Austrian Ministry of Science and Research, and Norbert Kailer, Institute for Educational Research for the Austrian Economy, 1991.

Canada

Co-ordinated and edited by Gilles Jasmin, Research and Information on Education Directorate, Department of the Secretary of State of Canada, 1992.

Denmark

Lavst Riemann Hansen, Danish Federation of Professional Associations, 1992.

Finland

Matti Parjanen, University of Tampere, 1991.

France

Hélène Ben Rekassa, Direction des Enseignements Supérieurs, ministère de l'Éducation nationale, Bruno Bordage, Service d'éducation permanente, Université de Rennes (in French only), 1992 (out of print).

Germany

Stefan Lullies and Ewald Berning and "Study on Flexible Organisation of Learning and Distance Study in the Federal Republic of Germany and in the Former German Democratic Republic", H.J. Back and J. Fichter, Institute for Development, Planning and Factual Research, University of Hanover, and W.D. Heider, German Ministry of Education and Science.

Italy

Sveva Avveduto and Roberto Moscati, National Research Council Institute for Studies on Scientific Research and Documentation, 1991.

Japan

Motohisa Kaneko, Research Institute for Higher Education, Hiroshima University, 1992.

Netherlands

Jorine E.M.B. Janssen, with an introduction by Paul van Oijen, Division for Future Studies on Higher Education and Research, Dutch Ministry of Education and Science, 1992.

Norway

Ellen Brandt, Institute for Studies in Research and Higher Education, 1991.

Portugal

M.J. Filipe Santos Oliveira, Professeur, Université nouvelle, Lisbon, 1992.

Sweden

Gunnar Ahlén and Marie Säll, Swedish Ministry of Education, Dan Andersson, Egon Hemlin and Vaike Pielbusch, National Swedish Board of Universities and Colleges, 1991.

Switzerland

Marcel Baeriswyl, deputy director, Banque cantonale de Berne, and Monika Roth-Herren, advocate Secrétaire Juridique de l'Association Suisse des Banquiers (1991) and "La formation professionnelle continue transfrontalière'', Joint OECD/Swiss authorities Seminar, Lugano 22-23 May 1991 (in French only), 1992.

United Kingdom

Keith Drake, University of Manchester.

United States

Dr. E. Stephen Hunt, Higher Education and Adult Learning Division, Office of Research, US Department of Education, 1992.

Former Yugoslavia

Professor Dusan Savisevic and Professor Goran Jovanovic, Belgrade University, 1991.

*
* *

Special contributions

Report of the Commission of European Communities, 1992.

Survey carried out with the contribution of the Business and Industry Advisory Committee (BIAC), ''Examen des formations continues dans quelques grandes entreprises'' (in French only), 1992.

Bibliography

BORDAGE, B. (1992), "Continuing University Education in France: A Dichotomous System", in *Higher Education Management,* Vol. 4, No. 1, OECD, Paris, March.

CANADA DEPARTMENT OF THE SECRETARY OF STATE (1989), *One in Every Five. A Survey of Adult Education in Canada,* a joint publication of Statistics Canada and Education Support Sector.

CANADA EMPLOYMENT AND IMMIGRATION DEPARTMENT (May 1987), *Adult Training Survey* (preliminary report).

CEREQ (1988), "Où en est l'effort de formation continue des entreprises?", *CEREQ-Bref,* Bulletin de Recherches, No. 32.

CERVERO, R. M. and AZZERETTO, J. F. (1990), *Visions for the Future of Continuing Professional Education,* University of Georgia.

COLARDYN, D. (1990), "The Challenge of Continuing Professional Education", *CRE-Action,* No. 4, Vol. 92, pp. 69-79.

COLLOQUIUM AT THE SORBONNE (April 1991), "Les enseignements de niveau supérieur et l'emploi", Paris.

COMMISSION OF EUROPEAN COMMUNITIES (1991), "Higher education in the European Community towards the year 2000", University of Siena, Ediun Coopergion Society Coop. A.R.L., Rome, July.

DEPARTMENT OF PHARMACY (1992), *Distance Learning in Industrial Pharmaceutical Sciences,* University of Manchester.

DORE, R. P. and SAKO, M. (1989), *How the Japanese Learn to Work,* Routledge, London.

ESNAULT, E. (1990), "Les universités et l'évolution de l'emploi", in *Compétences universitaires et industrie, CRE-Action,* No. 4, Vol. 92, pp. 23-28.

EURICH, N. P. (1990), *The Learning Industry: Education for Adult Workers,* The Carnegie Foundation for the Advancement of Teaching, New Jersey.

GÉHIN, J.-P. (1989), "L'évolution de la formation continue dans les secteurs d'activité (1973-1985)", *Formation et Emploi,* No. 25, pp. 19-35, Paris.

HEINKE, G. W. and WEIHS, H. H. (1990), "Continuing Education for Engineers in Canada", *International Journal of Applied Engineering Education,* Vol. 2, No. 5, pp. 254-274.

MADIGAN, K. (1990), "Further Education and Training and Collective Bargaining: The Experience of Five Countries", free document, OECD, Paris.

OECD (1975), *Recurrent Education: Trends and Issues,* Paris.

OECD (1977), *Learning Opportunities for Adults,* Vol. 1, Paris.

OECD (1982), *The University and the Community – The Problem of Changing Relationships,* Paris.

OECD (1984), *Industry and University: New Forms of Co-operation and Communication,* Paris.

OECD (1987*a*), *Adults in Higher Education,* Paris.

OECD (1987*b*), *Universities under Scrutiny,* Paris.

OECD (1988), *Facilities for Post-compulsory Education and Training,* Paris.

OECD (1989*a*), *Employment Outlook,* Paris.

OECD (1989*b*), "University-enterprise Relations in OECD Member Countries", Committee for Scientific and Technological Policy, Paris.

OECD (1989*c*), "Strengthening the Scientific and Technological Potential for Social and Economic Development: The Role of Higher Education", in *Education and the Economy in a Changing Society,* Paris.

OECD (1989*d*), *Japan at Work: Markets, Management and Flexibility,* Paris.

OECD (1990*a*), "Challenges and Opportunities in the 1990s", Statement by the Manpower and Social Affairs Committee, in *Labour Market Policies for the 1990s,* Paris.

OECD (1990*b*), *Education in OECD Countries 1987-88,* Paris.

OECD (1990*c*), Statement by the Yugoslav authorities at the meeting of the Education Committee at Ministerial level.

OECD (1990*d*), "Further Education and Training of the Labour Force", United Kingdom national report, free document, Paris.

OECD (1990*e*), "Assessment and Recognition of Skills and Competences: Developments in France", free document, Paris.

OECD (1991*a*), *Employment Outlook,* Paris.

OECD (1991*b*), *Alternatives to Universities,* Paris.

OECD (1992), "Rural Entrepreneurship: The Role of Institutions of Higher Learning in Fostering Job Creation and Economic Development in Rural America", in *Businesses and Jobs in the Rural World,* Paris.

OECD (1993), "The Flows of Graduates from Higher Education and their Entry into Working Life", in *Higher Education and Employment: Synthesis Report.*

PARRY, G. and WAKE, C. (eds.) (1990), *Access and Alternative Futures for Higher Education,* Hodder and Stoughton, London.

SCHULLER, T. (ed.) (1991), *The Future of Higher Education,* The Society for Research into Higher Education and Open University Press, Buckingham.

SLOWEY, M. (1991), "Assessment and Certification of Skills and Competences Acquired Following Initial Education and Training", unpublished, Newcastle-upon-Tyne University, United Kingdom.

SQUIRES, G. (1993), "The Role of the Humanities and Social Sciences in Professional Education", in *Higher Education and Employment: The Case of the Humanities and Social Sciences,* OECD, Paris.

SWISS AUTHORITIES (28 June 1989), *Message Concerning Special Measures in Favour of Continuing Training at Professional and University Levels.*

US DEPARTMENT OF EDUCATION (1985), *Trends in Adult Education 1964-1984,* Washington, DC.

US DEPARTMENT OF LABOR, BUREAU OF STATISTICS (1985), *How Workers Get their Training,* Washington, DC.

VAN VUGHT, F.A. (1989), *Governmental Strategies and Innovation in Higher Education,* Series 7, Kingsley, London.

VAUGHN, P. and SQUIRES, G. (1990), *Maintaining Professional Competence. A Survey of the Role of Professional Bodies in the Development of Credit-learning CPD Courses,* University of Hull, Hull.

WELSH, L. and WOODWARD, P. (1990), quoted by K. Drake in ''The Role of Continuing Professional Education in Higher Education in the United Kingdom'', free document, OECD, Paris.

MAIN SALES OUTLETS OF OECD PUBLICATIONS
PRINCIPAUX POINTS DE VENTE DES PUBLICATIONS DE L'OCDE

ARGENTINA – ARGENTINE
Carlos Hirsch S.R.L.
Galería Güemes, Florida 165, 4° Piso
1333 Buenos Aires   Tel. (1) 331.1787 y 331.2391
                       Telefax: (1) 331.1787

AUSTRALIA – AUSTRALIE
D.A. Information Services
648 Whitehorse Road, P.O.B 163
Mitcham, Victoria 3132   Tel. (03) 873.4411
                            Telefax: (03) 873.5679

AUSTRIA – AUTRICHE
Gerold & Co.
Graben 31
Wien I   Tel. (0222) 533.50.14
            Telefax: (0222) 512.47.31.29

BELGIUM – BELGIQUE
Jean De Lannoy
Avenue du Roi 202 Koningslaan
B-1060 Bruxelles   Tel. (02) 538.51.69/538.08.41
                     Telefax: (02) 538.08.41

CANADA
Renouf Publishing Company Ltd.
1294 Algoma Road
Ottawa, ON K1B 3W8   Tel. (613) 741.4333
                       Telefax: (613) 741.5439
Stores:
61 Sparks Street
Ottawa, ON K1P 5R1   Tel. (613) 238.8985
211 Yonge Street
Toronto, ON M5B 1M4   Tel. (416) 363.3171
                        Telefax: (416)363.59.63
Les Éditions La Liberté Inc.
3020 Chemin Sainte-Foy
Sainte-Foy, PQ G1X 3V6   Tel. (418) 658.3763
                           Telefax: (418) 658.3763

Federal Publications Inc.
165 University Avenue, Suite 701
Toronto, ON M5H 3B8   Tel. (416) 860.1611
                        Telefax: (416) 860.1608

Les Publications Fédérales
1185 Université
Montréal, QC H3B 3A7   Tel. (514) 954.1633
                         Telefax: (514) 954.1635

CHINA – CHINE
China National Publications Import
Export Corporation (CNPIEC)
16 Gongti E. Road, Chaoyang District
P.O. Box 88 or 50
Beijing 100704 PR   Tel. (01) 506.6688
                      Telefax: (01) 506.3101

CHINESE TAIPEI – TAIPEI CHINOIS
Good Faith Worldwide Int'l. Co. Ltd.
9th Floor, No. 118, Sec. 2
Chung Hsiao E. Road
Taipei   Tel. (02) 391.7396/391.7397
           Telefax: (02) 394.9176

CZECH REPUBLIC – RÉPUBLIQUE TCHÈQUE
Artia Pegas Press Ltd.
Narodni Trida 25
POB 825
111 21 Praha 1   Tel. 26.65.68
                   Telefax: 26.20.81

DENMARK – DANEMARK
Munksgaard Book and Subscription Service
35, Nørre Søgade, P.O. Box 2148
DK-1016 København K   Tel. (33) 12.85.70
                        Telefax: (33) 12.93.87

EGYPT – ÉGYPTE
Middle East Observer
41 Sherif Street
Cairo   Tel. 392.6919
           Telefax: 360-6804

FINLAND – FINLANDE
Akateeminen Kirjakauppa
Keskuskatu 1, P.O. Box 128
00100 Helsinki

Subscription Services/Agence d'abonnements :
P.O. Box 23
00371 Helsinki   Tel. (358 0) 121 4416
                   Telefax: (358 0) 121.4450

FRANCE
OECD/OCDE
Mail Orders/Commandes par correspondance:
2, rue André-Pascal
75775 Paris Cedex 16   Tel. (33-1) 45.24.82.00
                         Telefax: (33-1) 49.10.42.76
                         Telex: 640048 OCDE
Internet: Compte.PUBSINQ @ oecd.org
Orders via Minitel, France only/
Commandes par Minitel, France exclusivement :
36 15 OCDE

OECD Bookshop/Librairie de l'OCDE :
33, rue Octave-Feuillet
75016 Paris   Tel. (33-1) 45.24.81.81
                (33-1) 45.24.81.67

Documentation Française
29, quai Voltaire
75007 Paris   Tel. 40.15.70.00

Gibert Jeune (Droit-Économie)
6, place Saint-Michel
75006 Paris   Tel. 43.25.91.19

Librairie du Commerce International
10, avenue d'Iéna
75016 Paris   Tel. 40.73.34.60

Librairie Dunod
Université Paris-Dauphine
Place du Maréchal de Lattre de Tassigny
75016 Paris   Tel. (1) 44.05.40.13

Librairie Lavoisier
11, rue Lavoisier
75008 Paris   Tel. 42.65.39.95

Librairie L.G.D.J. - Montchrestien
20, rue Soufflot
75005 Paris   Tel. 46.33.89.85

Librairie des Sciences Politiques
30, rue Saint-Guillaume
75007 Paris   Tel. 45.48.36.02

P.U.F.
49, boulevard Saint-Michel
75005 Paris   Tel. 43.25.83.40

Librairie de l'Université
12a, rue Nazareth
13100 Aix-en-Provence   Tel. (16) 42.26.18.08

Documentation Française
165, rue Garibaldi
69003 Lyon   Tel. (16) 78.63.32.23

Librairie Decitre
29, place Bellecour
69002 Lyon   Tel. (16) 72.40.54.54

Librairie Sauramps
Le Triangle
34967 Montpellier Cedex 2   Tel. (16) 67.58.85.15
                            Tekefax: (16) 67.58.27.36

GERMANY – ALLEMAGNE
OECD Publications and Information Centre
August-Bebel-Allee 6
D-53175 Bonn   Tel. (0228) 959.120
                 Telefax: (0228) 959.12.17

GREECE – GRÈCE
Librairie Kauffmann
Mavrokordatou 9
106 78 Athens   Tel. (01) 32.55.321
                  Telefax: (01) 32.30.320

HONG-KONG
Swindon Book Co. Ltd.
Astoria Bldg. 3F
34 Ashley Road, Tsimshatsui
Kowloon, Hong Kong   Tel. 2376.2062
                       Telefax: 2376.0685

HUNGARY – HONGRIE
Euro Info Service
Margitsziget, Európa Ház
1138 Budapest   Tel. (1) 111.62.16
                  Telefax: (1) 111.60.61

ICELAND – ISLANDE
Mál Mog Menning
Laugavegi 18, Pósthólf 392
121 Reykjavik   Tel. (1) 552.4240
                  Telefax: (1) 562.3523

INDIA – INDE
Oxford Book and Stationery Co.
Scindia House
New Delhi 110001   Tel. (11) 331.5896/5308
                     Telefax: (11) 332.5993
17 Park Street
Calcutta 700016   Tel. 240832

INDONESIA – INDONÉSIE
Pdii-Lipi
P.O. Box 4298
Jakarta 12042   Tel. (21) 573.34.67
                  Telefax: (21) 573.34.67

IRELAND – IRLANDE
Government Supplies Agency
Publications Section
4/5 Harcourt Road
Dublin 2   Tel. 661.31.11
             Telefax: 475.27.60

ISRAEL
Praedicta
5 Shatner Street
P.O. Box 34030
Jerusalem 91430   Tel. (2) 52.84.90/1/2
                    Telefax: (2) 52.84.93

R.O.Y. International
P.O. Box 13056
Tel Aviv 61130   Tel. (3) 546 1423
                   Telefax: (3) 546 1442

Palestinian Authority/Middle East:
INDEX Information Services
P.O.B. 19502
Jerusalem   Tel. (2) 27.12.19
              Telefax: (2) 27.16.34

ITALY – ITALIE
Libreria Commissionaria Sansoni
Via Duca di Calabria 1/1
50125 Firenze   Tel. (055) 64.54.15
                  Telefax: (055) 64.12.57
Via Bartolini 29
20155 Milano   Tel. (02) 36.50.83

Editrice e Libreria Herder
Piazza Montecitorio 120
00186 Roma   Tel. 679.46.28
               Telefax: 678.47.51

Libreria Hoepli
Via Hoepli 5
20121 Milano   Tel. (02) 86.54.46
                 Telefax: (02) 805.28.86

Libreria Scientifica
Dott. Lucio de Biasio 'Aeiou'
Via Coronelli, 6
20146 Milano   Tel. (02) 48.95.45.52
                 Telefax: (02) 48.95.45.48

JAPAN – JAPON
OECD Publications and Information Centre
Landic Akasaka Building
2-3-4 Akasaka, Minato-ku
Tokyo 107   Tel. (81.3) 3586.2016
              Telefax: (81.3) 3584.7929

KOREA – CORÉE
Kyobo Book Centre Co. Ltd.
P.O. Box 1658, Kwang Hwa Moon
Seoul   Tel. 730.78.91
           Telefax: 735.00.30

**Ministry of Education & Training
MET Library
13th Floor, Mowat Block, Queen's Park
Toronto   M7A 1L2**

MALAYSIA – MALAISIE
University of Malaya Bookshop
University of Malaya
P.O. Box 1127, Jalan Pantai Baru
59700 Kuala Lumpur
Malaysia   Tel. 756.5000/756.5425
                            Telefax: 756.3246

MEXICO – MEXIQUE
Revistas y Periodicos Internacionales S.A. de C.V.
Florencia 57 - 1004
Mexico, D.F. 06600   Tel. 207.81.00
                            Telefax: 208.39.79

NETHERLANDS – PAYS-BAS
SDU Uitgeverij Plantijnstraat
Externe Fondsen
Postbus 20014
2500 EA's-Gravenhage   Tel. (070) 37.89.880
Voor bestellingen: Telefax: (070) 34.75.778

**NEW ZEALAND
NOUVELLE-ZÉLANDE**
GPLegislation Services
P.O. Box 12418
Thorndon, Wellington   Tel. (04) 496.5655
                            Telefax: (04) 496.5698

NORWAY – NORVÈGE
Narvesen Info Center – NIC
Bertrand Narvesens vei 2
P.O. Box 6125 Etterstad
0602 Oslo 6   Tel. (022) 57.33.00
                            Telefax: (022) 68.19.01

PAKISTAN
Mirza Book Agency
65 Shahrah Quaid-E-Azam
Lahore 54000   Tel. (42) 353.601
                            Telefax: (42) 231.730

PHILIPPINE – PHILIPPINES
International Book Center
5th Floor, Filipinas Life Bldg.
Ayala Avenue
Metro Manila   Tel. 81.96.76
                            Telex 23312 RHP PH

PORTUGAL
Livraria Portugal
Rua do Carmo 70-74
Apart. 2681
1200 Lisboa   Tel. (01) 347.49.82/5
                            Telefax: (01) 347.02.64

SINGAPORE – SINGAPOUR
Gower Asia Pacific Pte Ltd.
Golden Wheel Building
41, Kallang Pudding Road, No. 04-03
Singapore 1334   Tel. 741.5166
                            Telefax: 742.9356

SPAIN – ESPAGNE
Mundi-Prensa Libros S.A.
Castelló 37, Apartado 1223
Madrid 28001   Tel. (91) 431.33.99
                            Telefax: (91) 575.39.98

Libreria Internacional AEDOS
Consejo de Ciento 391
08009 – Barcelona   Tel. (93) 488.30.09
                            Telefax: (93) 487.76.59

Llibreria de la Generalitat
Palau Moja
Rambla dels Estudis, 118
08002 – Barcelona
              (Subscripcions) Tel. (93) 318.80.12
              (Publicacions) Tel. (93) 302.67.23
                            Telefax: (93) 412.18.54

SRI LANKA
Centre for Policy Research
c/o Colombo Agencies Ltd.
No. 300-304, Galle Road
Colombo 3   Tel. (1) 574240, 573551-2
                            Telefax: (1) 575394, 510711

SWEDEN – SUÈDE
Fritzes Customer Service
S–106 47 Stockholm   Tel. (08) 690.90.90
                            Telefax: (08) 20.50.21

Subscription Agency/Agence d'abonnements :
Wennergren-Williams Info AB
P.O. Box 1305
171 25 Solna   Tel. (08) 705.97.50
                            Telefax: (08) 27.00.71

SWITZERLAND – SUISSE
Maditec S.A. (Books and Periodicals - Livres
et périodiques)
Chemin des Palettes 4
Case postale 266
1020 Renens VD 1   Tel. (021) 635.08.65
                            Telefax: (021) 635.07.80

Librairie Payot S.A.
4, place Pépinet
CP 3212
1002 Lausanne   Tel. (021) 341.33.47
                            Telefax: (021) 341.33.45

Librairie Unilivres
6, rue de Candolle
1205 Genève   Tel. (022) 320.26.23
                            Telefax: (022) 329.73.18

Subscription Agency/Agence d'abonnements :
Dynapresse Marketing S.A.
38 avenue Vibert
1227 Carouge   Tel. (022) 308.07.89
                            Telefax: (022) 308.07.99

See also – Voir aussi :
OECD Publications and Information Centre
August-Bebel-Allee 6
D-53175 Bonn (Germany)   Tel. (0228) 959.120
                            Telefax: (0228) 959.12.17

THAILAND – THAÏLANDE
Suksit Siam Co. Ltd.
113, 115 Fuang Nakhon Rd.
Opp. Wat Rajbopith
Bangkok 10200   Tel. (662) 225.9531/2
                            Telefax: (662) 222.5188

TURKEY – TURQUIE
Kültür Yayinlari Is-Türk Ltd. Sti.
Atatürk Bulvari No. 191/Kat 13
Kavaklidere/Ankara   Tel. 428.11.40 Ext. 2458
Dolmabahce Cad. No. 29
Besiktas/Istanbul   Tel. (312) 260 7188
                            Telex: (312) 418 29 46

UNITED KINGDOM – ROYAUME-UNI
HMSO
Gen. enquiries   Tel. (171) 873 8496
Postal orders only:
P.O. Box 276, London SW8 5DT
Personal Callers HMSO Bookshop
49 High Holborn, London WC1V 6HB
                            Telefax: (171) 873 8416
Branches at: Belfast, Birmingham, Bristol,
Edinburgh, Manchester

UNITED STATES – ÉTATS-UNIS
OECD Publications and Information Center
2001 L Street N.W., Suite 650
Washington, D.C. 20036-4910 Tel. (202) 785.6323
                            Telefax: (202) 785.0350

VENEZUELA
Libreria del Este
Avda F. Miranda 52, Aptdo. 60337
Edificio Galipán
Caracas 106   Tel. 951.1705/951.2307/951.1297
                            Telegram: Libreste Caracas

Subscription to OECD periodicals may also be placed through main subscription agencies.

Les abonnements aux publications périodiques de l'OCDE peuvent être souscrits auprès des principales agences d'abonnement.

Orders and inquiries from countries where Distributors have not yet been appointed should be sent to: OECD Publications Service, 2 rue André-Pascal, 75775 Paris Cedex 16, France.

Les commandes provenant de pays où l'OCDE n'a pas encore désigné de distributeur peuvent être adressées à : OCDE, Service des Publications, 2, rue André-Pascal, 75775 Paris Cedex 16, France.

7-1995

OECD PUBLICATIONS, 2 rue André-Pascal, 75775 PARIS CEDEX 16
PRINTED IN FRANCE
(91 95 09 1) ISBN 92-64-14477-3 – No. 47961 1995